T0208509

The Way the Wind Blew

A History of the Weather Underground

•••

RON JACOBS

VERSO
London • New York

Dedicated to those who gave their lives
and freedom in the struggle against
racism and imperial war

First published by Verso 1997
© Ron Jacobs 1997
All rights reserved

3 5 7 9 10 8 6 4 2
Verso
UK: 6 Meard Street, London W1F 0EG
USA: 180 Varick Street, New York NY 10014-4606

Verso is the imprint of New Left Books

ISBN 978-1-85984-167-9

British Library Cataloguing in Publication Data
A catalogue record for this book is available from the British Library

Library of Congress Cataloging-in-Publication Data
A catalog record for this book is available from the Library of Congress

Typeset by M Rules in Baskerville
Printed by The Cromwell Press, Trowbridge, Wiltshire

Contents

List of Illustrations iv
List of Acronyms v
Preface and Acknowledgements vi

1... 1968: SDS Turns Left 1
2... Weather Dawns: The Break and the Statement 24
3... Into the Streets: Days of Rage 38
4... Down the Tunnel: Going Underground 66
5... Women, the Counter-culture, and the
Weather People 90
6... Changing Weather 127
7... A Second Wind? The *Prairie Fire* Statement 157
8... The End of the Tunnel: Weather and Its
Successors 170

Bibliography 188
A Weather Chronology 195
The Cast 203
Index 210

List of
Illustrations

Mark Rudd at Columbia University gym, 1968   10–11

Bill Ayers addressing a rally at Ann Arbor,
November 1968   14–15

SDS demonstration in Michigan, November 1968   16–17

Weather graffiti in New York City   47

Days of Rage organizing leaflet, October 1969   52

Demonstrators clash with police in Chicago,
October 1969   58–59

Bernadine Dohrn and Brian Flanagan outside court
in Chicago, October 1969   63

Class War comix, fall 1969   72

Cartoon illustrating the "Mobilization to end the
war in Vietnam," November 1969   76–79

Diana Oughton at an SDS convention in Flint,
Michigan, December 1969   80–81

Greenwich Village townhouse in which Weatherman
members died   96–97

Panther 21 support rally in New York, spring 1970   102–103

Communiqué about the New York City Police
HQ bombing, June 1970   110–111

FBI "WANTED" poster, 1970   112–113

Dianne Marie Donghi and Jane Spiegelman
outside court, July 1970   115

Mayday 1971 poster   134

New Morning "letterhead" and Prairie Fire logo   159

Breakthrough first-issue cover, March 1977   176

List of Acronyms

BLA	Black Liberation Army
CIA	Central Intelligence Agency
FBI	Federal Bureau of Investigation
JBAKC	John Brown Anti-Klan Organizing Committee
M2M	May 2nd Movement
Mobe	Mobilization to End the War in Vietnam
PFOC	Prairie Fire Organizing Committee
PLP/PL	Progressive Labor Party/Progressive Labor
RYM	Revolutionary Youth Movement, eventually split into RYM I and RYM II
SDS	Students for a Democratic Society
SLA	Symbionese Liberation Army
SNCC	Student Nonviolent Coordinating Committee
TDA	The Day After
WUO	Weather Underground Organization

Preface and Acknowledgements

I first became aware of Weatherman in the fall of 1970, after opening a copy of *Quicksilver Times* and reading about the group's assistance in Timothy Leary's escape from a prison in California. Although I personally preferred the antics of that other psychedelic prankster Ken Kesey, the fact that a political organization had aided the unreservedly apolitical Leary to escape fascinated me.

Then, at high school on a US military base in West Germany, where I was involved in organizing against the Vietnam war, I began reading as much as I could about Weatherman and its history. I found its politics difficult to understand but always admired its style and its ability to hit targets which in my view deserved to be hit. When I returned to the US after high school I floated in and out of organizations on the Left, where the presence of Weather was always felt, as an example both of commitment and of the necessity to organize deep popular support. My own political path has led me to shun military actions in favor of mass-based organizing, but I believe Weather's insistence on an anti-racist and anti-imperialist (and, belatedly, anti-sexist) analysis was fundamental to my political development.

The New Left was constantly changing, reacting to events in the world and in the movement itself. Many of today's critics view the Students for a Democratic Society of late 1968 and early 1969 (and afterwards) in relation to its original intentions as expressed in the Port Huron Statement. When they write about its history after the June 1969 convention, they often do so in terms of a betrayal of the ideals of the organization before it split. It is my contention that what happened at that convention and afterwards was not so much the end of the New Left as yet another sharp turn in the history of the Left itself. Another tendency in many writers is to relate this part of its history with an emphasis on the personalities involved and not the politics. While they are arguably intertwined, it is my hope that this text is primarily a political history of Weatherman, and not merely an account of personalities.

● ● ●

I would like to thank first and foremost Holly and Ian Thistle, who encouraged me to resume my writing and studies.

Next in line for thanks would have to be my family, especially my parents, who may disagree with my views but have always encouraged me to think.

Equally important, at least in regards to my writing, were Peter Bohmer and Nancy Allen, faculty of The Evergreen State College in Olympia, Washington, whose criticisms and encouragement carried me through the first of many drafts.

Thanks aplenty also to my editors at Verso: Sally Singer whose excellent editing work made this a book for all students of history; Michael Sprinker who gave me my first bit of hope that this story would reach more than just my friends; and Judith Ravenscroft, whose work in the final months of the editing process demanded of me a clarity essential to the story I wish to tell.

I also wish to thank Jim and Glenda Thistle for their unending support.

Without the excellent resources of The Evergreen State College Library I would have taken much longer to gather the necessary references, and without its extremely helpful staff – especially Brian, Andrea, and Louise – my momentary frustrations would have been more than momentary. I also thank Karen, Darryl, and Barb of the InterLibrary Loan staff at the Bailey-Howe Library of the University of Vermont, the folks at the Amherst College Library and the Labadie Collection at the University of Michigan, Amy Beth and the Lesbian Herstory Archives, Roz Payne and Joe Hudak.

Also, acknowledgements are extended to Roger Lippman, George Katsiaficas, Steve, and a couple of individuals who worked with members of Weather but prefer to remain completely anonymous, as well as various activists whose insights and conversation helped to shape my approach to this book.

And, then of course, my housemates in 1989-90: Dave, Leanne, Timothy, and Greg, and sometimes Howard – for being there and keeping me honest. Oh yeh, and Stephanie, too.

Every attempt has been made to ensure that all citations are complete. However, given the nature of the North American underground press, it has not always been possible to provide complete information, especially in the case of specific page numbers. Also, in the early chapters of the text, I refer to the New Left as such. However, as the lines between the New Left and Old Left become blurred, I use the more general term, the Left.

1...

1968:
SDS Turns Left

I send you, my friends, my best wishes for the New Year 1968.

As you all know, no Vietnamese has ever come to make trouble in the United States. Yet, half a million troops have been sent to South Vietnam who, together with over 700,000 puppet and satellite troops, are daily massacring Vietnamese people and burning and demolishing Vietnamese towns and villages.

In North Vietnam, thousands of US planes have dropped over 800,000 pounds of bombs, destroying schools, churches, hospitals, dikes and densely populated areas.

The US government has caused hundreds of thousands of US youths to die or be wounded in vain on Vietnam battlefields.

Each year, the US government spends tens of billions of dollars, the fruit of American people's sweat and toils, to wage war on Vietnam.

In a word, the US aggressors have not only committed crimes against Vietnam, they have also wasted US lives and riches, and stained the honor of the United States.

Friends, in struggling hard to make the US government stop its aggression in Vietnam, you are defending justice and, at the same time, you are giving us support.

To ensure our Fatherland's independence, freedom, and unity, with the desire to live in peace and friendship with all people the world over, including the American people, the entire Vietnamese people, united and of one mind, are determined to fight against the US imperialist aggressors. We enjoy the support of brothers and friends in the five continents. We shall win and so will you.

Thank you for your support for the Vietnamese people.

Ho Chi Minh [1]

The story of the Weather organization begins in 1968. From the Tet offensive of the national liberation forces in Vietnam to the assassination of Martin Luther King, Jr., to the uprisings in France and at Columbia University, to the invasion of Czechoslovakia and the Chicago Democratic convention – the events of that year created the political space for the emergence of this New Left organization – one arguably without precedent in United States history.

Within the United States the anti-racist and anti-war movements constituting the New Left, which had been growing in leaps and bounds since the late 1950s, took on thousands of new members in 1968, and began to develop a more radical approach in their analysis and activities. These approaches were partly reactions to the intensification of the war in Vietnam and a belief that a new "fascism" was on the rise in the United States. This fascism was manifested politically in a new concern over law and order and experienced socially in the increasing use of brutal police methods during protests and insurrections. For example, during the black rebellion following King's murder, Mayor Richard Daley of Chicago ordered the police to "shoot to kill" any looters.

The response of the New Left was to develop a more coherent stance toward the liberal–conservative establishment. No longer were particular racist policies or murderous acts protested; instead the New Left sought to acknowledge the totality of social and political injustice in the US, a system that it came to label as imperialist.

Students for a Democratic Society (SDS) – the national organization which, partly by design and partly by default, carried the mantle for the New Left in the United States – was at the forefront of this new perspective. The organization's paper, *New Left Notes*, became the forum for a discussion of how to combat US imperialism, in theory and practice – a discussion that sometimes became acrimonious and divisive. Within SDS itself an older, sectarian Marxist-Leninist group – then called the Progressive Labor Party but soon to shorten its name to Progressive Labor (PL) – formed its own power base[2]. Anti-nationalist and anti-Soviet, PL recruited mostly among students from the elite universities on the west and east coasts. It received its broadest support in 1965–7, when it formed the May 2nd Movement (M2M) against US involvement in Vietnam – the only national organization of its kind at the time. Its members' ability to manipulate discussion and votes at SDS national conventions and locally, and their knowledge of Left rhetoric and theory, enabled them to hold more power than their numbers warranted. Although a marginal faction at the beginning of 1968, by year's end PL had, if nothing else, created a division within SDS so deep that the rift between those who supported PL and those who didn't was irreparable.

In the January 15, 1968 issue of *New Left Notes* an article appeared entitled "Resistance and Repression." The article was an attempt to move SDS and its actions beyond "the point [where] it became necessary to define and confront the institutions of American aggression in Vietnam – [to] the point when it became necessary to start building a movement which could take over those institutions. Earlier demonstrations had "enabled [the movement] to show our strength, but did not give us forms to use that strength."[3] The events of 1968 and beyond were to change this, as SDS began to see itself as a revolutionary movement. No longer would the New Left merely react to America's exploitative and racist system, but, instead, it would provide an alternative vision.

On the evening of January 11, 1968, outside the Fairmount Hotel on San Francisco's Nob Hill, a picket line of hundreds marched on the sidewalk shouting slogans and bearing signs stating their opposition to US aggression in Vietnam. Inside the hotel Secretary of State Dean Rusk, one of the war's principal architects and apologists, addressed members of San Francisco's political and economic elite. As the crowd of picketers grew in size and volume, police in full riot gear amassed at one end of the block. Then, suddenly, the police were on top, around and among the demonstrators. With clubs flailing, the officers grabbed and beat protestors, before throwing them in the back of waiting paddy wagons. The initial responses of the demonstrators "were shock, amazement, fear, and then, anger." According to Karen Wald, a reporter for *New Left Notes*, "the fear was too great for any attempt to rescue . . . anyone who was grabbed." The following day, Wald realized, like many of her fellow activists, that this was repression at its most raw. The days were "long gone when you had to be seeking arrest . . . in order to be busted." No longer, she wrote, would the state allow forms of protest it did not agree with. No longer would the state treat those whom it considered dangerous as anything less than dangerous.[4]

Those who shared this opinion concluded that the only effective protest action was one not permitted by those in power. In this context, any state-sanctioned demonstration was automatically suspect. Herbert Marcuse, a controversial Marxist philosopher and professor at San Jose State University in California, termed such state tolerance of opposition "repressive tolerance." By this he meant that by allowing certain non-confrontational forms of dissent, the state could continue its policies while providing a safety valve for those who disagreed with them. This safety valve placated the opposition without challenging the power of the state.

The Rusk demonstration was not the first instance of police violence against protestors – the Oakland Stop the Draft Week protests and the demonstrations at the Pentagon in October 1967 are two other examples. The Stop the Draft protests were attempts to block access to the Oakland induction center, at first by using such tactics as demonstrators linking arms across streets leading to the center, and then, after police viciously attacked them, by blocking the streets with their bodies, junked cars, trash cans, and whatever else might be handy. Once police moved into an area to clear it, protestors left that particular part of the street and repeated their tactics in another spot. The massive anti-war demonstration at the Pentagon was also put down violently, and the brutal tactics of the police on that occasion seemed to mark the intensification of a strategy which demanded that the state attack any demonstrations it did not approve of, no matter what their style or size.

The Fairmount police attack intensified the struggle over tactics within the movement. In its discussions and newspapers, SDS began to distinguish between moral reactions and political reactions. Although a reaction stemming from moral outrage might be militant, its symbolic nature meant that it was not seen as something that could change the reality of war or racism. Instead, such actions merely petitioned the perpetrators of those crimes to repent and remedy their ways. The morally outraged demonstrator acted from the belief that the moral rightness of his/her position would be recognized and would ultimately convince the target of the protest to change for the better.

This moral approach was contrasted to a political one, that is, a strategy which sought to impart a revolutionary consciousness to the activist. Such a consciousness-building effort "demanded that [the anti-war and anti-racist movements] transcend the difficult but inevitable boundary between symbolic and effective action."[5] In other words, one shouldn't just petition the system to change itself in response to moral rebukes, but should build an alternative by actively fighting the system.

The attempts by the SDS to dichotomize between morally motivated and politically motivated actions seems, in retrospect, diversionary. The history of social movements shows that, no matter what the designs of the individuals involved, such groups develop organically and usually adopt a synthesis of the two approaches.

Another facet of the larger debate taking place within SDS concerned the merits of educating to organize versus acting to organize. Differences over this question deepened the split in the movement. Proponents of educational organizing – primarily members of Progressive Labor – insisted that an educational approach strengthened anti-imperialist forces and, without such a base, militant actions could isolate and eventually weaken the movement. Proponents of action, on the other hand, argued that militancy and the police response to it played a key role in organizing efforts because they revealed the repressive nature of the state and its agencies. In the violent culture of the United States, the argument went, only violence made any impact. For newly politicized white American youth, this was a revelation.

Members of Ann Arbor SDS (calling themselves the Jesse James Gang) – notably Bill Ayers, Jim Mellen, and Terry Robbins – argued that militant tactics also "provide[d] activity based on an elan and a community which show[ed] young people that we *can* make a difference, we *can* hope to change the system, and also that life within the radical movement can be liberated, fulfilling, and meaningful."[6] Echoing the policy of the Student Nonviolent Coordinating Committee (SNCC), these three insisted that there was no dichotomy between confrontation and organizing, a position also favored by the Black Panther Party. The experiences of activists during the Columbia University strike in late spring would further validate this perspective within SDS.

Then there's the sort of feeling among some of us that the revolutionary classes, the Vietnamese, the black people, the oppressed, are the ones who are going to make history. We're not going to stand on

the side of the oppressors. We're going to align ourselves with the
oppressed. That's why the Vietcong flags were there in the buildings.

Mark Rudd[7]

If there was any event in 1968 in the United States which demonstrated to SDS not only the legitimacy of the action theory, but also the developing internationalist consciousness of the American New Left, it was the student uprising at Columbia University. The issues involved were directly related to US domestic and foreign policies. Columbia's decision to continue with its ill-advised plan to build a gymnasium in Morningside Park in the black Harlem neighborhood near to the university infuriated community leaders, the student body, and local residents who had requested through official means and street rallies that Columbia cancel its plans. The university's response was to provide a rear door to the gym allowing restricted access to neighborhood residents. Not only did this smack of Jim Crow, but it illustrated quite graphically the university's perception of itself as the dominant force in the community, free to do whatever it wished; a perfect metaphor for the United States' view of its role in the world.

The other issue which provoked the uprising concerned the university's involvement with the Institute for Defense Analysis (IDA). The Institute was funded by the federal government which used the facilities of twelve private universities for weapons research and counter-insurgency and riot-control studies. In the fall of 1967, a letter written by the 100-member Columbia chapter of SDS and signed by hundreds of students asked the university's president Grayson Kirk to end the school's participation in the IDA program. The petition was ignored. When questioned about his failure to respond, Kirk replied that the letter did not carry a return address.

Columbia's refusal to acknowledge its complicity in the twin evils of US society – racism and imperialism – and to reconsider its position forced radicals into fighting back with a one-two combination of their own. On April 23, 1968, they marched to Low Library, which housed the university administrative offices, and demanded that charges be dropped against students placed on disciplinary probation because of an earlier protest against IDA. Three of the students on probation were Mark Rudd, a member of SDS since 1966; John Jacobs (known as JJ), a former PL member who had single-handedly led a sit-in against CIA recruiting at Columbia the previous school year; and Ted Gold, a junior at Columbia who had been arrested earlier in the year at a demonstration in New York against Secretary of State Dean Rusk, a week after Rusk spoke in San Francisco.

When the students found their way blocked by right-wing counter-demonstrators, some protestors left the area and marched to the gym construction site where a struggle with police ensued. Part of the fence surrounding the site was torn down in the melee, and one student was arrested. After this incident, students and supporters marched back to campus and took over first one, and then eventually four, buildings. As the occupation/liberation continued, almost everyone on campus and, for that matter, in the country, came to know what was going on and why. A week after the first building, Hamilton Hall, was taken over, the police attacked, vindicating "the strikers, [by] proving that the administration was more willing to have students arrested and beat-up and to disrupt the university than to stop its policies of exploitation, racism, and support for imperialism."[8] A strike ensued, effectively shutting down the university for the rest of the semester. Two more violent mass arrests occurred: one on May 17 in an

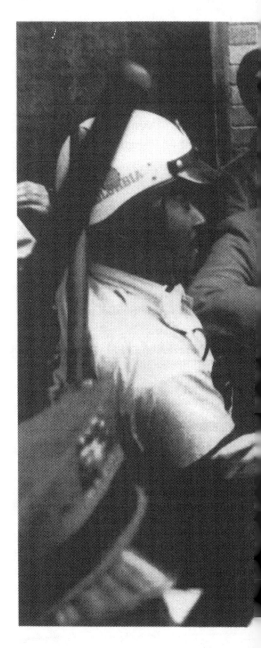

Mark Rudd tries to force
his way into the gym at
Columbia University, 1968.
Rudd, having spent seven
years in hiding, finally
surrendered to the authorities in September 1977
to answer charges relating
to his leadership of
Weather Underground
and his earlier actions at
Columbia. Photograph
reproduced courtesy of
UPI-Bettmann.

apartment building owned by Columbia, which was in the process of evicting tenants to make way for higher-income housing, and the other on May 21, at Hamilton Hall, after those whom the media labeled as leaders of the rebellion were suspended and 120 people attempted to "liberate" the building in support of those students and their demands. A total of 712 students and others were arrested during the course of the strike. Members of the New York chapter of the National Lawyers' Guild immediately set to work on the court cases. Among these lawyers and paralegals was Bernardine Dohrn, who was to be National Secretary of SDS in 1968–9 and a central figure within Weather.

Within the "liberated" buildings themselves, the students and their allies adopted a new way of life that, in a sense, embodied the revolution they had talked about for so long. Hours were spent in discussion of tactics, politics, and logistics. In addition, for most of the participants this was the first time in their lives that they had had power, to use or abuse. For most such a realization was a liberating experience and an expression of the sense of elan and community which Ayers, Mellen, and Robbins of Ann Arbor SDS had written of.

• • •

Primary among the theoretical questions begging resolution in SDS policy was the role of racism in US society and how best to combat it. As the organization struggled to develop a potentially revolutionary ideology, the race issue came to be as important as opposition to the Vietnam war. However, it was infinitely more divisive. At stake was the question of how best to organize black people in the United States: as super-exploited members of the working class (PL's position) or as an internal colony within the United States. One's position on this question depended largely on one's opinion of the Black Panther Party, at the time the most revolutionary group within the black struggle. Those who opposed PL politically did so primarily because they believed, like the Panthers, that blacks in the United States constituted a colony and, as such, had a right to national self-determination.

The argument revealed fundamental differences of opinion over the role of nationalism in the liberation of a people. To PL and its supporters, all nationalism was seen as diversionary and subject to manipulation by the bourgeoisie of the colony. For most of the other members of SDS, though, there was a vital difference between nationalism and national liberation and, for the black community in the United States, the Panthers represented a revolutionary road to national liberation. Bernardine Dohrn emphasized the Panther stance on this issue in an article entitled "White Mother Country Radicals," in *New Left Notes*. Dohrn wrote that "[the Panthers] have been open and aggressive opponents of black capitalism . . . and firm supporters of the line that anti-capitalism is fundamental to black liberation." Further on in the article, Dohrn elaborated on an earlier SDS statement, made after the shootings by police of black students attempting to desegregate a bowling alley in Orangeburg, South Carolina: "The best thing that we can be doing for ourselves, as well as for the Panthers and the revolutionary black liberation struggle is to build a fucking white revolutionary movement."[9] This would become one of Weatherman's first goals.

The question of nationalism was also involved in the matter of Vietnam. Did one support the National Liberation Front in its revolutionary struggle for self-determination (the anti-PL position), or only because it was being attacked by the United

Bill Ayers addresses a rally at Ann Arbor, Michigan, in November 1968. Ayers, one of the leaders of the Jesse James Gang (a faction of SDS) at the University of Michigan and at one time Diana Oughton's boyfriend, was protesting the alleged mistreatment of a university student. Photograph reproduced courtesy of UPI-Bettmann.

In November 1968, the University of Michigan chapter of SDS paraded through downtown Ann Arbor and past the university campus, calling for a student strike in protest of the Vietnam war. Pictured just to the right of the car are (left to right) Diana Oughton, Bill Ayers and Milton "Skip" Taube. Photograph reproduced courtesy of UPI-Bettmann.

States (the PL position)? As the year rolled on, and into 1969, the questions of nationalism, differences in class analysis, and perceptions of youth culture would determine the fate of SDS and create the opening from which Weatherman would emerge.

As for youth culture, SDS was focusing most of its energies on those youth who were working on the presidential campaign of Senator Eugene McCarthy of Wisconsin. His anti-war stance and appeal to college students made the campaign the natural place for SDS to organize, given their predominantly student membership. Although SDS had little faith in electoral politics, they worked with other organizations planning mass demonstrations at the upcoming Democratic Party convention in Chicago. The best known of these groups was the Youth International Party, or Yippies, founded by radicals Abbie Hoffman, Jerry Rubin, Anita Hoffman, Nancy Kurshan, and Paul Krassner. Their behavior during convention week – including public insults of Mayor Daley, the nomination of a pig for president, the verbal and physical assault of police officers – and the reaction they provoked from Chicago police would change SDS politics.

SDS's experiences that week not only caused them to shift their organizational emphasis from the McCarthy youth to those already in the streets, they also provided many in the organization with a glimpse of the revolutionary potential of the counter-culture. This, in turn, brought about a synthesis between the developing class analysis in the SDS and the burgeoning youth culture. Early attempts at producing such a synthesis began with the observation that a class is defined by its relationship to the means of production and, as the young do not control any of those means, they should identify themselves with the oppressed, not out of guilt but out of self-interest. Even the interests of privileged students (who constituted most of SDS at the time) lay more with anti-capitalist forces, not because they needed to work, but because of monopoly capitalism's alienating expectations and requirements.

The first attempt at this synthesis can be found in a statement submitted by Mike Klonsky, a former national president of SDS, respected for his knowledge of Marxist-Leninist theory and reasoned arguments against PL. The statement, adopted at the December 1968 national convention in Ann Arbor, was entitled "Towards a Revolutionary Youth Movement." It was an attempt not so much to present youth (specifically students) as working-class, but more to "build a link through working-class youth to the working class to bring the dynamic of the student movement to the workers."[10] Klonsky emphasized that it was necessary for SDS to expand beyond its student base into the working class. Such an effort would be facilitated by the cross-class nature of the youth culture of the 1960s and its denial of what it saw as alienating effects of American life.

Although youth itself was not intrinsically revolutionary, Klonsky believed that "by developing roots within the class struggle, [it could be] insured that the movement would not be reactionary."[11] Youth, the argument went, would add militancy to the struggle once it merged with the working class. The younger members of that class would be the focus of the organizing effort, not because they were more oppressed, but because they felt that oppression, in the form of the military draft, low-wage jobs, and schooling that seemed irrelevant to their experience, differently from their elders. In addition, the youth culture, in its opposition to the system, had already laid a base for such an effort.

What this expansion of the organization would necessarily mean was an end to privileges associated with being students (draft deferments); an intensified struggle against racism within the movement and the youth culture; and a redirection of organizing efforts toward technical schools, community colleges, and high schools and away from the colleges of privilege in which the movement had been born.

"Towards a Revolutionary Youth Movement" is evidence of the substantive changes which occurred in SDS in 1968, and within six months it had split the organization. It would also be a major impetus to the formation of Weatherman.

Debate over both the nationalism and the youth culture questions continued into the next year. A PL racism proposal passed at the December 1968 convention which labeled all types of nationalism reactionary was overturned at a National Council meeting in March 1969 in favor of a resolution by the anti-PL forces in support of the Black Panther Party. In another victory for the anti-PL forces, a PL-sponsored resolution condemning the use of marijuana and psychedelics, and, by inference, youth culture, was also defeated.

A proposal by Bill Ayers and Jim Mellen presented at the March 1969 National Council, entitled "Hot Town, Summer in the City," was subsequently adopted in place of the PL statement on drugs. For the most part the proposal was a refinement of Klonsky's "Towards a Revolutionary Youth Movement," but there were a few substantive changes. Among these were the observations that the repression of youth culture seemed to have an inversely proportionate effect to its growth, and that there were no class boundaries to its repression, although working-class youth, especially those of color, suffered most. This recognition enhanced the view that although all workers were oppressed, youth endured a different kind of oppression. The statement went on to list some of the special forms this oppression took: the draft, mandatory and irrelevant schooling, and lack of job opportunities and meaningful employment. This proposal, like Klonsky's, was part of a growing strategy by SDS to shift its recruiting focus away from college students and toward youth in general, including high-school and community-college students, youth in the army or who were otherwise employed, and those young people who had "dropped out" of society. The proposal searched for ways to involve less privileged youth than those found in most universities in the movement against war and racism.

Another area of concern for Ayers and Mellen was the black liberation movement. Once again, the vanguard role of the Black Panther Party was emphasized, as was the continued rise in police surveillance and repression of the Panthers' activities. Their proposal condemned the "absence of substantial support – power – by the white movement" for facilitating this repression and urged the "white movement to be a conscious, organized, mobilized fighting force capable of giving real support to the black liberation struggle."[12] To create such a consciousness, it was necessary for SDS to organise youth according to the Revolutionary Youth Movement's analysis, that is, not as a cultural phenomenon but as members of the working class who had experienced "proletarianization" in schools and the army.[13] In these institutions, the young found themselves in the same boat as the oppressed black community, slaves to the lords of war and industry.

• • •

In the late 1960s, SDS could not ignore the evidence of the feminist movement that was gaining momentum in US society. Within SDS itself, the more revolutionary the members became, the more the women activists became conscious of their limited role in the organization. Susan Stern, an SDS member then working and living in Seattle, remarked that "SDS was operating at half of its potential" because of its failure to give women leadership positions.[14] The growing awareness that women in the movement "do office work and even run offices, but are discouraged from articulating political positions or taking organizational leadership" caused many women to rethink their participation in the movement and question its integrity. [15] Some women claimed men were to blame for their oppression. Others saw the system of power as the culprit: pitting gender against gender to keep people divided. Some voiced the possibility of considering women as a separate class, while others, citing the example of the revolutionary Vietnamese women, quoted NFL theorists: "The struggle of women for freedom and equality could not but identify itself with the common struggle for national liberation" [16] – or, simply, the common struggle.

Some women eventually left SDS for other organizations, many of them separatist in nature. Most, however, hoped, as Naomi Jaffe, a *New Left Notes* staffer in New York, and Bernardine Dohrn did, that a new strategy could be developed. This strategy for liberation did "not demand equal jobs, but meaningful creative activity for all; not a larger share of the power, but the abolition of commodity tyranny; not equally reified sexual roles but an end to sexual objectification and exploitation; not equal aggressive leadership in the movement, but the initiation of a new style of non-dominating leadership."[17] If nothing else, SDS and the New Left movement would, it was hoped, redefine the nature of a white-male-dominated society.

NOTES

1. Ho Chi Minh, "New Year, 1968", *The Sixties Papers*, ed. Judith Clavier Albert and Stewart Albert, Praeger, New York, 1984.

2. The Progressive Labor Party (PL) formed as the result of a split in the Communist Party–USA (CPUSA) after Krushchev's renunciation of Stalin and the subsequent division between the Chinese and Soviet parties. Although never very large, PL exacted an influence way beyond its numbers in the New Left.

3. *New Left Notes*, January 15, 1968.

4. Karen Wald, "Dan Rusk at the Fairmount: A View from One Corner," *New Left Notes*, January 22, 1968, p. 30. Seven organizers of the Stop the Draft Week protests were indicted for a variety of charges connected with the Oakland demonstrations. They became popularly known as the Oakland Seven. Hundreds were arrested and beaten at the Pentagon demonstration during attempts by police and federal marshals to clear the Pentagon grounds.

5. Richard Fried, Jerome Hoffman and James Tarlau (Princeton SDS), "Potentials and Limitations of the Student Movement: 1967–1968," *New Left Notes*, February 5, 1968.

6. B. Ayers, J. Mellen, and T. Robbins, "Ann Arbor SDS Splits," *New Left Notes*, October 7, 1968, p. 4.

7. Quoted in Joanne Grant, *Confrontation on Campus: The Columbia Pattern for the New Protest*, New American Library, New York, 1969.

8. Ibid., p. 243.

9. Bernardine Dohrn, "White Mother Country Radicals," *New Left Notes*, July 29, 1968.

10. Mike Klonsky and others, "Towards a Revolutionary Youth Movement," *New Left Notes*, December 31, 1968.

11. Ibid.

12. Students for a Democratic Society, "The Black Panther Party: Towards the Liberation of a Colony," *New Left Notes*, April 4, 1969.

13. Jim Mellen, "More on Youth Movement," *New Left Notes*, May 13, 1969.

14. Ibid., p. 42.

15. M. Welb, "Women, We Have a Common Enemy," *Washington Free Press*, Summer 1968.

16. B. Dohrn, "Liberation of Vietnamese Women," *New Left Notes*, October 25, 1968.

17. B. Dohrn and Naomi Jaffe, "You Got the Look," *New Left Notes*, March 18, 1968.

2...

Weather Dawns: The Break and the Statement

If white people are going to claim to be white revolutionaries or white mother country radicals, [they] should arm themselves and support the colonies around the world in their just struggle against imperialism.

Huey Newton[1]

The 1969 SDS National Convention began on June 18. By evening, over 2,000 members had passed through the security and underground-media cordon to take their places in the Chicago Coliseum. Discussion among many of the non-PL members centered on the statement which had appeared in that day's issue of *New Left Notes*, entitled "You Don't Need a Weatherman to Know Which Way the Wind Blows . . ." The piece, which was written primarily by members of the Columbia chapter of SDS, borrowed its title from the Bob

Dylan song, "Subterranean Homesick Blues." It was the founding statement of the Weatherman organization.

The Weatherman statement had been discussed and argued about in SDS national and regional offices since the late spring. Its primary drafters included SDS members whose names would become synonymous with Weather: Bill Ayers, Mark Rudd, Bernardine Dohrn, Jim Mellen, Terry Robbins, John Jacobs, and Jeff Jones. The other authors were Karin Ashley, Howie Machtinger, Gerry Long, and Steve Tappis. Ashley and Tappis would cease to be Weather members before the end of the year.

As delegates argued over the contents of the Weatherman statement, and PL members figured out a strategy for maintaining some degree of power in the organization, a group of Black Panthers entered the hall. One of them launched into a tirade against PL, calling the group "counterrevolutionary traitors." At first those who were listening applauded or booed the speaker depending on their political views, but when the speech slipped into a rant against the growing feminist movement, the noise died down. Then another Panther began to chant "Pussy power, Pussy power!" and asserted that the only position for a woman in the revolution was a prone one. These statements provoked a very loud reaction from virtually everyone on the floor, and the Panthers eventually left the podium, having lost any voice for the time being.

The next day began much the same as the first, with discussions and workshops continuing throughout the meeting space. Toward evening, while members argued over a number of resolutions on racism, a group of Panthers once again entered the hall and took the stage. They read a statement repeating much of the previous night's comments about PL and told SDS that they would be judged by their actions – in effect calling for SDS to expel PL from its ranks. A number of PL members then grabbed the microphone and attacked the Panther position on black nationalism, while otherwise praising them. In addition, they accused the SDS leadership of opportunism in bringing the Panthers to the convention. Next, Bernardine Dohrn took the stage and asked those in the hall if it was still possible to work in the same organization as PL. Mark Rudd then called for an adjournment, but before debate could begin on the motion, Dohrn led about half the delegates to the adjacent annex where the discussion continued through the night.

Meanwhile, those who remained in the main hall also continued to talk and, some eighteen hours later, issued a resolution calling for unity. Finally, by midnight on the 21st, debate ended and the delegates who had left with Dohrn the previous night filed back into the main hall and listened to Bernardine read PL out of SDS. PL members tried unsuccessfully to shout her down with cries of "Shame" and "Smash racism!" Once the reading of the expulsion resolution was over, the new SDS, without PL, marched out of the hall with their fists in the air.

When the convention ended next day not only was PL no longer officially recognized, but, despite the existence of a third force at the convention, which came to be known as RYM (Revolutionary Youth Movement) II, the national office now comprised Weatherman members Bill Ayers, Jeff Jones, and Mark Rudd. The newly formed coalition between RYM II and Weatherman, based mostly on their opposition to PL, was tenuous, to say the least.

The only resolution to pass through this fractious convention besides the ouster of PL was a call for a week of protests in Chicago in the fall. The composition of the organizing committee for these protests also reflected Weatherman's new power: Kathy Boudin, Bernardine Dohrn, Terry Robbins, the three national officers, and Mike Klonsky of RYM II.

With the publication of "You Don't Need a Weatherman to Know Which Way the Wind Blows," Bernardine Dohrn's call a year earlier for a white fighting force to support the black liberation movement began its transition from words·into reality. If the statement did little else, it placed the struggle of black people in the United States at the forefront of the fight against US imperialism.

The statement identified the black struggle as part of the "worldwide fight against US imperialism," and argued that the black community's role in that struggle was of primary importance. If the black community (or colony, as Weather preferred to call it) was successful in its fight for liberation, the United States would not survive because of the essential role played by the citizens of the black colony in the formation and perpetuation of the US system. Slavery was fundamental to the development of capitalist society in the British colonies and in the first several decades of the United States: not only did the slave trade create profits which could be invested elsewhere, it also enabled slaveowners to acquire wealth rapidly. When slavery was no longer essential to the continued accumulation of wealth, the ex-slaves and their descendants were relegated to a no less essential but often harsher economic slavery which existed to this day.[2]

By defining the black community as a colony "existing in the country as a whole" instead of solely as a black-belt nation in the southern United States (an analysis advanced by Robert Williams and the Movement for a Republic of New Afrika),[3] the statement perceived the "common historical experience of importation and slavery and caste oppression" as the basis for national identity. That identity, as the "Black Proletarian Colony," made it essential for the colony to organize as revolutionary socialists. Attempts to organize black people in other ways denied the struggle's communist roots. Although it differed from that of many black nationalist groups, Weatherman's analysis was virtually identical to that of the Panthers, especially in terms of its insistence on black Americans' history of economic oppression.

"You Don't Need a Weatherman" went on to argue that it was "necessary for black people to organize separately and determine their actions separately" from their white counterparts.[4] To do otherwise denied the struggle's particular investment in the defeat of US imperialism and negated its revolutionary nature, a sentiment that echoed previous struggles within the black liberation movement, especially those surrounding the ouster of whites from SNCC in 1965. As Stokely Carmichael wrote in his book, *Black Power*: "black people must run their own organizations because only black people can convey the revolutionary idea – and it is a revolutionary idea – that black people are able to do things themselves."[5] The authors of "You Don't Need a Weatherman" concluded the section on the black liberation movement by stating that although the black movement did not need white revolutionary allies to win, it would be racist to contend: "1) that blacks shouldn't go ahead making the revolution or 2) that they should go ahead alone with making it." Instead, the statement argued that a third path, supporting the black struggle, should be taken.

While few in the revolutionary New Left disputed the central role of the black liberation struggle in the fight against US imperialism, many critics of Weatherman warned against creating an organization which would act primarily in support of the black struggle. Paul Glusman, in an article in the New Left journal *Ramparts*, offered the opinion that, "SDS, all of it . . . left out any mention of white youth as a revolutionary force for themselves . . . One would think the Panthers would prefer allies who are in it for themselves and not guilt-ridden successors to the civil-rights liberals who left when things got hot."[6] David Hilliard of the Panthers expanded this criticism in a statement made after the Panther-sponsored United Front Against Fascism conference in Oakland, California in June 1969.[7] This statement was a response to a Weatherman offer to help participants at the conference distribute a petition calling for community control of the police in communities of color but not in white communities. Such an offer assumed that white communities would not liberalize their police forces while communities of color would. Besides expressing a lack of faith in white people, young and old, the Weatherman offer seemed to imply that the third-world community was not able to do the work itself.

After its discussion of the role of the black anti-imperialist struggle in the overthrow of the US system, "You Don't Need a Weatherman" addressed the question of united-front politics. That is, whether it was desirable first to create a broad democratic coalition to throw out imperialism and then, after that task was completed, to install socialism. It was the opinion of Weatherman that this two-step process was usually applied to semi-feudal societies and was unnecessary in the United States which was in the most advanced stage of capitalism: imperialism. When imperialism was defeated in the United States, Weather argued, it would be replaced with socialism, and nothing else. While many on the revolutionary New Left agreed with this analysis, they did not agree with Weatherman's interpretation that working with reform movements in a united front, no matter what the cause, was counter-revolutionary. It was here that Weatherman disagreed with most of the rest of the revolutionary left, RYM II included. Weatherman's insistence on revolutionary purity – or, as "You Don't Need a Weatherman" put it, "someone not for revolution is not actually for defeating imperialism either" – created a situation which, in the long run, made it virtually impossible to organize anyone but the already converted.

In the international fight against US imperialism Weatherman supported all struggles for self-determination in the colonies. They reasoned that the cost to the imperialists increased proportionately with the support given to those struggles which, in turn, would lead to cutbacks in social-services spending and job creation at home. These cutbacks would force welfare recipients, and the working class in general, to struggle even harder to maintain a minimal standard of living. This, theoretically, would create a revolutionary situation which, if properly organized, would lead to the defeat of the ruling elites.

To realize such a vision, however, required the organization of the working class into a revolutionary force. In order to accomplish this, the working class had to be made aware that its interests lay with the anti-imperialist forces of the world – not a simple task in 1960s America. Although a few unions supported the more liberal demands of the anti-war movement (negotiations, for example, and an end to the bombing), most did not. Of those that did, very few of their members considered themselves revolutionaries. Consequently, SDS, and especially Weatherman, perceived white workers in the United States as only too happy to support the country's interventionist and racist program. Weatherman believed the white working class to be racist, pro-war, incapable of recognizing its own oppression, and the enemy of the anti-imperialist cause.

There was hope, however, for youth. Because of their current oppression especially in the form of the military draft, Weatherman decided it was possible to build a revolutionary youth movement, an idea that had originally been proposed in December 1968 in the statement "Towards a Revolutionary Youth Movement." Youth met the criterion that any person who had nothing but his or her own labor to sell was a member of the working class. Because they generally held a smaller stake than their elders in the existing society and had grown up "experiencing the crises of imperialism" – Vietnam, Cuba, black liberation – young people were more open to new ideas, especially the idea that the system could be overthrown. After all, thousands of young men were monthly being coerced into fighting for that system and had good reason to be rid of it.

The system, under threat, resorted more and more to force and an accompanying authoritarian ideology which – the statement continued – met with resistance, first from the black people of the United States and eventually from Chicano, Puerto Rican, and white youth as well. Some resisted through political struggle, many others – no matter what their class origin – by rejecting mainstream society and joining the counter-culture, which by now had developed a fighting edge due to its repression by the police. Calling themselves "freaks" and "yippies," counter-culture adherents were beaten up by the police for their anti-social behavior just as politicos were at demonstrations. When the two elements of youthful resistance joined together in a common fight, as in the ill-fated attempt by students, radicals, and counter-cultural street people to build People's Park in Berkeley in May 1969, an armed attack by police resulted, with the death in that instance of one protestor and the maiming of many others.

The developing youth movement transcended class. However, since the oppression of youth hit working-class youth hardest, it was necessary, as stated earlier in "Towards a Revolutionary Youth Movement," to move "from a predominantly student elite base to more oppressed [less privileged] youth" in order to expand the existing revolutionary force. To do this, the Weatherman statement emphasized the necessity of linking people's everyday crises to revolutionary consciousness. Weatherman gave as examples of a multi-issue approach the Columbia occupation of 1968, when the expansion into the black community surrounding Columbia was linked to the university's involvement in Defense Department counter-insurgency programs, and the battle over People's Park in Berkeley in 1969, where the question of private property came together with the issue of free speech and the concerns of the anti-war movement. Weatherman also urged students not to fight for reforms in the schools, but to close them down until the time came when schools could serve the people and not the corporate class.

Toward the end of the statement, Weatherman addressed the role of the police. In a section entitled "RYM and the Pigs," the police were defined not as representatives of the state, but literal embodiments of it. Given their ever-increasing aggression against radical groups (e.g. the raids on both the SDS and the Panther offices in Chicago and the shootings at People's Park in Berkeley in the spring of 1969), Weather believed that a revolutionary movement had to overcome the police or risk becoming "irrelevant, revisionist, or dead."

Of course, whether the primary aim was to fight the police or to attack the system which employed them, the state's repression of its opponents was bound to increase. As a result, it was necessary to oppose repression, which would "require the invincible strength of the mass base at a high level of active participation." In other words, "the most important task for [SDS] toward making the revolution . . . is the creation of a mass revolutionary movement, without which a clandestine revolutionary party would be impossible." It is unfortunate that Weatherman failed to adhere to its own advice and, like the Panthers, develop allies outside the revolutionary movement.

Most of "You Don't Need a Weatherman" is a more complex development of positions proposed in "Towards a Revolutionary Youth Movement." One topic remained unexamined in both: the role of women and of feminism in the revolutionary youth movement. Although two women were among its drafters, "You Don't Need a Weatherman" merely stated that the group had "a very limited understanding of the tie-up between imperialism and the women question." While acknowledging the continually expanding wage differential in the workplace based on gender and the gradual disintegration of the nuclear family under monopoly capitalism, the Weatherman leadership collectively stated that it "had no answer, but recognize[d] the real reactionary danger of women's groups that are not self-consciously revolutionary and anti-imperialist." They then proposed developing different forms of organization and leadership which would enable women to take on new, independent roles.

● ● ●

Although few Weatherman members prided themselves on their reading of political theory, seemingly preferring to draw their theory from praxis (Rudd is even quoted in Kirkpatrick Sale's account of SDS [1973] as bragging that he hadn't read a book in a year), one book which was widely read in the collectives was Régis Debray's handbook of guerrilla warfare in Latin America, *Revolution in the Revolution?* The importance to Weatherman of Debray's book is impossible to overstate. In addition to underground newspapers and other Left periodicals, well-thumbed copies of *Revolution in the Revolution?* were to be found in every Weather collective's house.

Nominally a handbook for the revolutionaries in South America, *Revolution in the Revolution?* was adopted by the future members of Weatherman in the interim between the Columbia strike and the June 1969 SDS convention probably because of its discussion of recent events in the Americas, and its mention of, and the author's familiarity with, the heroes of the New Left: Che Guevara and Fidel Castro. Although supposedly a guide to revolution, Debray seems to invalidate his purpose in the book in the first fifteen or so pages by stating that the Cuban revolution could not be repeated in Latin America or anywhere else. This was so, said Debray, because no revolution can copy another, but can only utilize the objective conditions within the particular country – conditions which, are "neither natural or obvious . . . [but] require years of sacrifice to discover."[8]

Patience was the strategy that Debray emphasized above all others. Quoting from the work of Simon Bolivar, he writes that the most valuable lesson for revolutionaries is tenacity. It is tenacity, after all, which provides the revolutionary with the foresight to see beyond the various failures and victories (s)he will encounter, as Debray learnt from his own experiences and his knowledge of the history of Cuban struggle against Batista. Failure, according to Debray, provides experience and knowledge far more than victory does.

Whether or not Weatherman accepted this concept in practice is questionable. It did, however, believe itself to have a clear answer to the ultimate question for a revolutionary organization: "How to overthrow the capitalist state?"[9] Its answer was to obey Debray's instructions in accordance with its self-perception. In contrast to the Panthers, Weatherman did not consider itself a self-defense force. Instead, it preferred the idea of forming the core of a future revolutionary army which, according to Debray, needed to exist as an organic unit separate from the regular population. In order to attain its goal, then, the revolutionary guerrilla army needed to be clandestine and, to show its viability, willing to take the initiative by attacking the enemy.

To maintain the necessary secrecy, Debray suggested operating in small autonomous groups or focos. These focos would develop their own strategy of attack to achieve an objective set out by a centralized leadership. Such a structure enabled each foco to carry out its part of the mission; however, if any member or members were captured, their knowledge of the entire operation would be limited to the movements of their particular foco. This structure also provided the organization itself with greater internal security as an infiltrator's knowledge would be severely limited.

While the focos carried out their work, continued Debray, the masses must be educated politically. Armed struggle alone would leave the revolutionary forces isolated. On the other hand, political struggle without armed action was equally undesirable, as a political organization risked becoming an end in itself, perhaps even becoming involved in the electoral process of the state. The moment, historically speaking, when political, military, and other considerations were ripe must be seized. How one determines such a moment came not from the understanding of a particular theory or terrain, but from "a combination of political and social circumstances" which, when recognized, could be acted upon.

All of which is not to say there should be no action before that historical moment. Indeed, wrote Debray, the revolution is a constantly changing reality. The occasional well-planned attack can convert more people to the idea of revolution than months of speeches and writings – a view borne out, for example, by the actions at Columbia, which radicalized many more people than previous rallies and speeches had done, thus substantially propelling the movement forward.

In order to facilitate the organization of the people, the revolutionary group must be strengthened and develop a truly mass line. If the group develops the correct line, the people will recognize it as the vanguard party. Should the party be composed of members of the bourgeoisie and the petty bourgeoisie, like Weatherman, and the masses accept their leadership, the members must "commit suicide as a class" in order to be reborn as workers.[10]

As long as no armed struggle exists, according to Debray, there can be no vanguard. Instead, what usually occurs in such a vacuum is the growth of a plethora of groups who call themselves Marxist-Leninist and revolutionary. Thus, in the late 1960s and early 1970s there were constant battles in the US between various sectarian groups over issues and tactics in a struggle, with each claiming to be more revolutionary than the others. Mass organizations such as the Seattle Liberation Front, November Action Coalition (Boston – Cambridge), the Mayday

Tribe (Washington, D.C.), and the People's Coalition for Peace and Justice attempted to lead the movement but, due largely to the lack of a long-term program and law enforcement harassment, fell by the wayside. In the interim, revolutionary organizations with a potential for longevity disintegrated into sectarian squabbles over marginal political issues. Weatherman recognized the danger of sectarianism because of its ongoing battle with the Progressive Labor faction in SDS. But although the organization wished to transcend such divisions by acting on Debray's advice and "pass(ing) over to the attack," its puerile focus on revolutionary purity undermined its aims and contributed to its failure to organize large numbers of people.[11]

NOTES

1. "Huey Newton Speaks on White Organizers," in *The Black Panthers Speak*, ed. Philip S. Foner, Lippincott, Philadelphia, 1970.
2. K. Ashley, B. Ayers, B. Dohrn, J. Jacobs, J. Jones, G. Long, H. Machtinger, J. Mellen, T. Robbins, M. Rudd, S. Tappis, "You Don't Need a Weatherman," *New Left Notes*, June 18, 1969. These and any quotes not otherwise noted are from this statement.
3. The idea of a separate black nation forming in the southern United States continues to be part of the program of some Left and nationalist groups today.
4. The idea of blacks working separately was first expressed within the New Left by Stokely Carmichael and others in the Student Non-Violent Coordinating Committee (SNCC). SDS was merely reaffirming this position in regard to their new revolutionary road.
5. S. Carmichael and C. Hamilton, *Black Power: The Politics of Liberation in America*, Vintage, New York, 1967, p. 42.
6. Paul Glusman, "More Mao Than Thou," *Ramparts*, Noah's Ark, Berkeley, September 1969.
7. David Hilliard, "Lumpen Proletarianism and Bourgeois Reactionarism," *The Black Panther*, August 9, 1969.
8. Régis Debray, *Revolution in the Revolution?*, Grove Press, New York, 1967, p. 20.
9. Ibid., p. 24.
10. Amilcar Cabral, quoted ibid., p. 112.
11. Ibid., p. 55.

3...

Into the Streets: Days of Rage

It has been almost a year since the Democratic Convention, when thousands of young people came together in Chicago and tore up pig city for five days. The action was a response to the crisis this system is facing as a result of the war, the demand by black people for liberation, and the ever-growing reality that this system just can't make it. This fall, people are coming back to Chicago: more powerful, better organized, and more together than we were last August. SDS is calling for a National Action in Chicago October 8–11. We are coming back to Chicago, and we are going to bring those we left behind last year.

SDS leaflet, summer 1969

After the convention in June 1969, Weatherman and RYM II controlled the new SDS, although they probably represented no more than 4,000 members of an organization whose membership in late 1968 had peaked at about 100,000. Their task was clear – to organize thousands of youths to come to Chicago and demonstrate "against the war in Vietnam, in support of the Black Panther Party, and in solidarity with all political prisoners, including Black Panther Huey P. Newton, and the eight under attack for last summer's righteous demonstrations" during the Democratic Party convention.[1] But with the National Organizing Committee for the fall protests composed of members of both Weatherman and RYM II, the stage was set for yet another split, even if no one thought so at the time.

Weatherman and RYM II were unified in their opposition to PL, mostly because of its attacks on the Black Panther Party, and black nationalism in general, and its criticism of the NLF and North Vietnam's willingness to negotiate an end to the war. But any lasting unity between the two was unlikely because they disagreed on almost everything else, especially strategy. Both believed that armed revolution was necessary in the United States, but the timing of that revolution and the role of white workers in it were a source of much discord. By late August, Mike Klonsky, nominal leader of RYM II, quit the National Organizing Committee, primarily because of his opposition to Weatherman's dismissal of the white working class as hopelessly reactionary. This left both the National Organizing Committee and the National Office completely in the hands of Weather. Bill Ayers, Mark Rudd, and Jeff Jones headed up the National Office, while the committee organizing the fall protests comprised Bernardine Dohrn, Terry Robbins, Kathy Boudin, and the three national officers.

RYM II regarded the call for massive demonstrations in the fall as a call for a "united front against imperialism" which would, by linking workers' struggles with the war in Vietnam and the black colonies, convince "the masses of working people" to take a stand against imperialism.[2] Given Weatherman's belief that united-front politics were not necessary in the United States because of its late stage of capitalist development, this issue was another point of dispute.

Also, according to Weatherman, any efforts to reform the system – the schools, workplace, army, etc. – were merely attempts to gain more privileges for the already privileged white population. As Mark Rudd and Terry Robbins put it in their reply to Klonsky's public letter of resignation: "Here [in the United States] the just struggles of the people do not necessarily raise consciousness or build a revolutionary movement. Much to the contrary, they often obscure the differences between the colony and the mother country, obscure white skin privilege, obscure internationalism."[3] Klonsky's view was that the working class must be won over by addressing their issues "with patience, not arrogance," and he and the rest of RYM II began organizing their own fall protests in Chicago.[4]

According to Weather chronicler Harold Jacobs (1970), Weatherman had not given up hope of realizing white America's revolutionary potential, but the general perception in the New Left in 1969 was that it had. Consequently, its isolation from the movement had begun.

If there is a conspiracy to end the war, if there is a conspiracy to end racism, if there is a conspiracy to end the harassment of the cultural revolution, then, we too, must join the conspiracy.

Ad in The Seed *to defend the conspiracy*

The so-called conspiracy referred to the indictment of eight men – the Chicago 8 – under new federal conspiracy statutes for, among other charges, "crossing state lines with the intent to riot" during demonstrations in Chicago at the time of the Democratic Party convention in August 1968. By including counter-cultural revolutionaries Abbie Hoffman and Jerry Rubin in the conspiracy indictment, the state demonstrated its perception of the counter-culture as insurrectionary. It is possible that by indicting the two yippies the Justice Department hoped to intimidate young people into forsaking revolutionary politics and life styles. Instead, the opposite happened. Chicago 8 defendant Tom Hayden capsulized the sentiment of a substantial number of the nation's youth with the statement, "Our identity is on trial."[5] The Chicago Conspiracy became a cause célèbre and as a result thousands of youth adopted revolutionary politics. Weatherman, hoping to gain recruits from this phenomenon, shifted toward support of counter-cultural struggles such as that in Berkeley over People's Park.

In Seattle, after police attacked a free rock concert at a local beach on August 10, a youth uprising lasting two nights took place in the university district, with massive looting and attacks against small businesses like record and clothing stores ("hip" capitalists) as well as buildings housing branches of national corporations. The local Weather collective encouraged attacks on banks, military recruiters, and other obvious targets connected to the war in Vietnam, as collectives would do in other cities where youth fought the police.

As the uprising in Seattle spread and black and Latino youths joined in, racist remarks were heard from some of the rioting white youth, to the distress of Weather members. Considering the centrality of racism to Weather's analysis and its oft-repeated insistence on the necessity to combat racism wherever it was found, its involvement with youth, especially white working-class youth spouting anti-black sentiments, increasingly led some members to further question the usefulness of organizing whites. Others in the New Left faced similar dilemmas regarding racism in the counter-culture but were willing to work and struggle with the racist attitudes they encountered, while Weather simply labeled as "pigs" all those it regarded as less politically advanced.

The counter-cultural watershed of the summer of 1969 was the Woodstock festival in August. Despite the input of some radical activists in the planning of the event, the weekend concert was primarily set up by the large record companies (notably Warner Brothers) to expand their markets, but the eventual breakdown of festival security created a liberating situation. A reporter for the Chicago underground paper *The Seed* wrote about it thus: "Woodstock was . . . a massive pilgrimage to an electrified holy land where high energy communism replaced capitalism . . . because the immediate negative forces of the outside world, cops, rules, and prices had been removed or destroyed."[6] The news that half a million young people had created their own society, no matter how temporary, convinced millions who didn't attend that a great counter-cultural community existed beyond whatever locality they happened to live in.

Before the festival the number of young people who embraced some aspect of the counter-culture – even if that meant merely buying records – was appreciated mainly by the entertainment industry. The sheer impact of the Woodstock festival on US society forced those in other segments of the American power structure to pay attention to youth as well. The New Left too took note. *New Left Notes* commented that the same record companies that "sell liberating music are big-time defense contractors," and argued that America's youth should liberate its culture. In the same manner that Weather linked so-called "hip" capitalists with corporate ones, the article informed readers that capitalists, not performers, made most of the money from music (soon after, of course, things changed, with entertainers often making more money than many small corporations). This was a commonly held analysis among counter-cultural radicals but would not be enough to convince the youth of America to join Weather in Chicago in the fall.[7]

• • •

Weatherman took the offensive once the members of the various collectives had returned to their cities of operation after the national convention. They believed that the best way to show their willingness to fight a revolution was to do just that, a view deriving not only from the Weather interpretation of the foco strategy, but also from its romanticized perception of US working-class youth. Cathy Wilkerson, a founder member, recalled that Weather "was trying to reach white youth on the basis of their most reactionary macho instinct, intellectuals playing at working-class toughs."[8] Indeed, Mark Rudd and Terry Robbins stated that Weather needed to be "a movement that fights, not just talks about fighting. The aggressiveness, seriousness, and toughness . . . will attract vast numbers of working-class youth."[9] With this class-based vision of an army, Weatherman and its approximately 350 members took its call for a revolution in Chicago to the youth of the nation.

In a highly publicized organizational effort one Saturday in July, Detroit Weatherman (or Motor City Weatherman, as the members referred to it) went to Metro Beach, located in a working-class suburb and at the time a favorite hangout for the youth of the area. Weatherman arrived in the early afternoon, carrying a red flag and distributing leaflets calling on youth to go to Chicago in October to fight the police. Within minutes of the group's arrival, a crowd of approximately two hundred had formed. They began arguing with the Weather cadre about communism, the Viet Cong, and racism in the United States. A short time later, after being informed that lifeguards had called the local sheriffs, Motor City Weatherman moved away to regroup and decide what to do next. The crowd had other ideas. Fists began to fly, and after a fierce fight, Weather left. It is doubtful that any of those on the beach that day ever went to Chicago, but one biker involved in the brawl later told a member of the Motor City collective that while he enjoyed the fight that afternoon, he "would enjoy fighting the pigs in Chicago more."[10]

Another action by Motor City Weatherman took place at a junior college, in an "all white working class community" according to *New Left Notes*. Weather's rationale for this target was that the students at the college were being trained for low-level managerial jobs that would directly oppress black people. A group of nine women "entered the classroom chanting, and barricaded the door with the teacher's desk. Various members of the cadre spoke to the students, who had been taking a final exam, about the Chicago action, imperialism, racism, and the oppression of women." After listening for a few minutes and growing increasingly angry because their exam was being interrupted, some male students pushed the Weather women out of the way in an attempt to leave. A fight ensued. The women failed to escape before the police arrived, and nine were arrested and charged with disorderly conduct.[11]

During this period local collectives functioned autonomously with regards to fundraising and actions around local issues. The national leadership (or Weatherbureau, as it came to be called) directed the individual collectives in terms of political positions and organization for the national action. Collectives maintained themselves financially by various means. Some members still received checks from their trust funds or relatives. Others worked regular jobs, sold drugs, or received public assistance, and some of those who were still in college obtained some kind of financial aid. All of these monies were placed in a common fund in each collective from which expenses were paid. The Weatherbureau supplemented its own collective income with whatever membership payments and contributions it received as the nominal leadership of SDS, which by this time was not much. In fact, several pleas for money were sent out in the fall of 1969 because of SDS's severe shortage of cash.

In tandem with external organizing actions the collectives also attempted to crush any vestiges of bourgeois ideology among members. To facilitate this, the national leaders, who were based in Chicago, traveled to Weather collectives around the country. Once there, the individual from the national leadership, say Rudd or JJ (John Jacobs), began a series of maneuvers designed to identify those local members perceived to be the most willing to cooperate with the leadership and place them in positions of power. This might involve marathon criticism sessions in which all those present, sometimes having ingested LSD, challenged the commitment of the person being critiqued. The procedure might include sexual activity designed to destroy monogamous relationships, whether equal partnerships or not, though some members agreed that their relationships needed to be redefined, and separated willingly, or the forced coupling of people who might or might not wish to sleep together. One purpose behind these procedures was to create a tightly run, autonomous, and ego-less foco of street fighters. Another, less obvious purpose was to decrease the power of locally strong individuals who might interfere with the overall plans of the national leadership. Weather's opposition to monogamy was based on the belief that it prevented members from taking risks and that the desire to protect the relationship would cause a failure of will. Doing away with traditional forms of monogamy was not necessarily a bad idea and formed part of a strategy to end male supremacist attitudes in the organization, but the authoritarian manner in which it was undertaken caused much useless dissension and emotional stress.

If the national leadership had paid closer attention to its less political counterparts in the counter-culture, perhaps it would have learned that new forms of relating to another – sexually and otherwise – are much easier to adopt if introduced with sensitivity and love. Instead, during this period the national leadership, using recruits eager to curry favor, destroyed strong monogamous associations by separating couples and ridiculing their relationships. The justification for these activities was the African revolutionary Amilcar Cabral's dictum of the necessity to "commit suicide as a class" in order to truly lead the revolution.

Weatherman graffiti in New York City. Clearly visible are the Weatherman logo and an iconic Vietcong fighter on a tomb-shaped piece of stone and, underneath, the text "MAKE PIGS PAY". Photograph from the collection of Will Miller, reproduced courtesy of *Liberated Guardian*.

• • •

Weather organized around the line that anyone "who played pig" was the enemy.[12] What Weather meant by the phrase was explained by Rudd in *New Left Notes*. His argument went like this: in order to maintain control, the ruling elites in the US utilized both "the priest and the hangman;" and, if the non-violent persuasion of the priest did not work, then the hangman's skills were employed to maintain order. To allow the teacher or the serviceman or woman off the hook just because they might be well-intentioned victims of circumstance was to allow the bourgeoisie to go unchallenged, and, in Weather's view, this was not much different from letting President Nixon off the hook for the continuing war in Vietnam.[13]

Accordingly, a group of Boston Weather people invaded a meeting in the early fall of 1969 at Boston University, which was called to organize anti-war actions coinciding with the October 15 Moratorium to End the War and the November 15 Mobilization to End the War. After barricading the doors, various members of the collective spoke for a few minutes and then attacked those present, calling them counter-revolutionaries and pigs because they differed with Weatherman's program and did not support its national action planned for Chicago.[14] Another action of the Boston Weather collective that fall was a raid on the Center for International Affairs at Harvard University. This government-funded institute, directed by a man named Benjamin Brown, was involved in war-related research. The Weather people "broke into the building, hung the Viet Cong flag from the window," attacked Mr. Brown and some of his colleagues, and then left. Three Weather men – Eric Mann, Henry Olson and Phil Nies – were charged for the attack.[15]

Its line on "playing pig," especially in relation to the blossoming GI movement for civil rights in the military and against the war, was more self-defeating for Weather than any of its other theoretical mutations. In every revolution victory has depended on large numbers of common soldiers. In its haste to make revolution, and without regard to the economic or social pressures on those in the military or facing the draft, Weatherman issued an ultimatum to the American soldiers. "Turn your gun around," it said, "or you are the enemy."[16] In essence, GIs were "pigs" until they proved otherwise. Ironically, as Carl Davidson of RYM II, pointed out, Weather's heroes, the National Liberation Front of Vietnam, who had "every reason to express a burning hatred of GIs never refer[red] to them with anything approximating the term 'pig.'"[17]

The approach of other Left groups shows how removed Weatherman's perspective was from that of the rest of the movement. About this time, *The Black Panther*, the party paper, printed weekly articles on the radical GI movement and addressed open letters to GIs calling for their support. Other anti-imperialist organizations printed special leaflets to give to GIs at demonstrations, especially when the demonstrations were held at military bases. These leaflets were sympathetic in tone and usually provided phone numbers and addresses of groups and individuals who might be of assistance to soldiers wishing to desert.

Recruiting for Weather at this time mostly involved getting young people interested in the actions planned for October in Chicago. Weather usually drew attention to itself by provoking some kind of reaction to its presence. Afterwards, those who expressed an interest in what Weatherman was or what they hoped to do, were invited either to the next planned action or to a meeting with members of the local collective at a neutral place – a coffee shop or restaurant, for example. Larry Grathwohl, an informer, was recruited into Weather in this way. After a couple of conversations in the streets of Cincinnati, about the war and the need for revolution in the US, with members of the local Weather collective, he accompanied the group to some demonstrations. They then invited him on a late-night graffiti-writing excursion and, finally, to the house the collective shared. After that visit, he was then asked to live in a house whose occupants functioned as a support group for the primary collective. His housemates in that house were allies of Weather but were not considered to be completely committed to the organization. Later he moved into the main Cincinnati collective's house, when the move was approved by visiting members of the Weatherbureau.[18]

Organizing for the Chicago demonstrations continued for the rest of the summer and fall. On September 4, in Pittsburgh, a group of eighty or so women from Weatherman collectives around the country ran through a high school shouting "jailbreak" and urged students to decide whether they were for the black and Vietnamese revolutions or against them. When the police appeared, the women fought viciously and broke away, only for twenty-six of them to be arrested down the road a few minutes later. According to the women's post-action summary, the demonstration proved that a "fighting force of women" existed, and, by existing, challenged male supremacy.[19]

Meanwhile, some members of Weather – including Bernardine Dohrn, Ted Gold of Columbia, Dianne Donghi of Cincinnati, Diana Oughton of Ann Arbor, and Eleanor Raskin of New York – traveled to Cuba to meet with representatives of the Cuban and North Vietnamese governments and the NLF of Vietnam. The trip lasted five weeks and involved tours of the Cuban countryside, long discussions, and even some work in the Cuban sugar fields. Although the FBI and its conservative supporters in the US Congress were convinced the trip was for "guerrilla training," little evidence other than hearsay exists to support this belief. However, Weatherman was told to raise the level of confrontation in the US in order to help the NLF and North Vietnamese win in Vietnam. Some of the travelers received rings made from the wreckage of B-52 bombers shot down over Vietnam. Nothing concrete came of the meetings but the inspiration they provided intensified the group's commitment to the struggle of the Vietnamese people and to a revolution in the United States.

• • •

As October 8 edged closer, Weatherman increased its efforts in cities throughout America, claiming that tens of thousands of youths would converge on Chicago "to tear the motherfucker apart."[20] The local collectives worked to obtain commitments from non-Weather radicals who had expressed previous interest in the upcoming actions, as the Weatherbureau stepped up its pressure on the local collectives to produce numbers. Collectives were located in New York, Boston, Seattle, the San Francisco Bay area, and a dozen or so cities and college towns in the Midwest – Cincinnati, Cleveland, Ann Arbor, Chicago, and Detroit were some of the larger contingents. Preparing for the worst, the city of Chicago cancelled all police leave and enforced overtime. National Guard troops were also placed on alert, in case they were needed by Illinois state officials.[21] In Seattle, cars belonging to

A leaflet advertising the SDS-organized Days of Rage, October 11, 1969. From the author's private collection.

members of the Weatherman collective were shot up by plain-clothes police in an attempt to intimidate the owners. Also in Seattle, the women of the Weather collective trashed a university building which housed the campus Reserve Officers Training Corps (ROTC).

Many groups in the movement advised supporters to stay away from Chicago and criticized the upcoming Weatherman action as adventurist and self-destructive. Fred Hampton of the Chicago Panthers observed, "The Weathermen should have spent their time organizing the white working and lumpen class instead of prematurely engaging in combat with trigger-happy pigs."[22] *The Seed* provided its readers with a preview of both the Weatherman and the RYM II actions (set to occur during the same week). The latter were coordinated with those of the Chicago Panthers and the local chapter of the revolutionary Latino organization, the Young Lords. The article included *The Seed*'s skeptical observation that although Weatherman was counting on thousands of youths to show up, its plans had failed to excite even the Chicago counter-culture and New Left communities.[23]

Other underground papers also reported on preparations in the various local Weather collectives. Members were taught self-defense and street-fighting techniques to calm their fears. Sympathetic doctors and first-aid workers helped with medical preparations, and those planning to attend the week of actions were advised to dress appropriately with protective gear like football helmets and padding.

Along with self-defense practice came an increasing display of bravado. In a speech to fellow Weather members at the Midwest National Action conference in Cleveland that August, Bill Ayers answered charges of adventurism from the Panthers and others by claiming that "if it is a worldwide struggle . . . then it is the case that nothing we could do in the mother country could be adventurist . . . because there is a war going on already." Ayers insisted that Weatherman was intent on opening another front in the worldwide revolution, and placed all those who disagreed with its ideas in the camp of "right-wingers [who] . . . are not our base, they never were, and they never could be." In response to RYM II's organizing slogan, "Serve the People," Ayers said that Weather would "fight the people" if to do so would further the international revolution. [24] A writer for the Boston underground paper *Old Mole* wrote at the time that "Weatherman [was] probably correct in denying that there will be a purely internal [domestic] revolution," but its actions did not "serve the needs of oppressed peoples – American or Vietnamese – but of frustrated people in the movement."[25]

Two days before Weatherman's October 8 debut a dynamite explosion destroyed a 10-foot statue of a policeman in Haymarket square where the "mass march" was to begin later in the week. The statue commemorated policemen who died during the 1886 Haymarket riot.[26]

Weatherman and its followers began to arrive in Chicago on October 6, two days before the actions were scheduled to begin. The churches and seminary buildings that were to serve as "movement centers" did not open until the following day, and the Weatherbureau had to find beds for supporters elsewhere that night. On the Wednesday evening, the 8th, members of the new revolutionary army attended an opening rally in Lincoln Park. Estimates of numbers ranged from 100 to 800. The crowd included hardened activists with years of movement experience, working- and lower-class youth from the Chicago area, and fresh-faced high-school kids from different parts of the country, as well as a sprinkling of counter-cultural street people and undercover cops from a variety of law-enforcement agencies. The crowd was prepared for confrontation. Most wore heavy steel-toed boots for kicking and were armed with clubs or short pieces of a type of steel bar used to reinforce poured concrete. Virtually all carried motorcycle or football helmets for protection, and wore gloves and clothing (primarily black) which covered as much of their skin as possible to protect them from mace or other chemical agents that the police might use.

Foremost in Weather members' minds was the question of numbers. As the zero hour approached, it became evident that there would not be tens of thousands of fighting youths in the streets that night. Still, there was hope that more than a few hundred would show up. And as these few hundred stood around a bonfire in the park waiting for the leadership collective to appear, they could not help but notice the large numbers of battle-ready police in the streets surrounding the park.

At last the leadership appeared, in camouflage fatigues, and the speechmaking began. Acknowledging that fewer than a thousand people had turned up at the rally, the speakers appealed to those present as the only non-racist whites in America and the only true revolutionaries willing to put their lives on the line to fight the Chicago police. In fact, only two weeks earlier, a few thousand activists had fought the police in the same park after a demonstration against the Chicago 8 trial. Three of the Chicago 8 defendants – Yippie Abbie Hoffman, anti-war activist John Froines, and former SDS leader Tom Hayden – were in the crowd that night. Hayden was the only one to speak, telling the crowd, "We are glad to see people back in Lincoln Park. We are glad to see the level of militancy increased."[27] Hoffman and Froines declined to address the crowd, and all three left after Hayden's short talk.

Despite the disappointing turn-out, the crowd responded to the speakers' appeal to their commitment to the Weather approach to revolution, so that, after an hour or two, "the odds didn't matter to most."[28] By the time the code word Marion Delgado was uttered, those present were ready to attack. (Delgado was a 5-year-old Chicano boy who had derailed a train in Alameda County, California by placing a slab of concrete on the rail, and his name had been chosen because of his half-mythic/half-joke status in Weatherman.)

Weather ran down the streets of Chicago toward the city's rich section, the Gold Coast, screaming and chanting, and catching the police off guard. "Windows were smashed . . . ," remembered Shin'ya Ono. "Small groups of ten, fifteen pigs on the way were taken by surprise and were totally powerless against the surging battalion. Some pigs were overpowered and vamped on severely. Within a few minutes all of us lost whatever fear and doubts we had before . . . Each one of us felt the soldier in us."[29]

After twenty minutes or so, and eight blocks away from the starting point of the rampage, the cops recovered and began their counter-attack, fighting viciously with both men and women, and using clubs, mace, tear gas, and guns. While some of the Weather people's violence was directed at obvious and not so obvious perpetrators of violence against the peoples of the world (banks and corporate offices), much of it was totally random and pointless. For example, windows of cars and apartments were smashed and, in one reported instance, a man trying to protect his Volkswagen was beaten severely, although he escaped without being hospitalized. After two protestors attacked a policeman and beat him unconscious, another officer shot one of them in the neck.

By 11.30 p.m., the street fighting had ended, with Weather in disarray. The rest of the night was spent attempting to get back to the various movement centers without being arrested, while the police reinforced their patrols. A resident of Chicago described the scene: "You couldn't walk anywhere without seeing cops. They were on every street corner in groups of two or three, sometimes with dogs. When you got off a bus, you could feel their eyes watching you all the way down the block 'til the next group of cops started watching you. They were in control."[30] The casualties for the night were 75 arrests and 21 officers and an unknown number of Weather people and bystanders injured, including at least three Weather people with police-inflicted gunshot wounds.

The following morning Weather nursed its wounds and reviewed the night's action. Many people from the West Coast collectives at first complained that they had been misled about the expected number of attendants. After several rounds of discussion, however, most of them accepted that the low numbers were as much their responsibility as anyone else's and the matter was dropped.

The national leaders realized that the other collectives were unwilling to criticize them (out of fear or fatigue) and took it upon themselves to open up their own self-criticism session. Analysing the possible reasons for the small turnout, they came to some of the same conclusions that the rest of the New Left had arrived at weeks earlier. According to the Weatherbureau the primary reasons for the low turnout at the Days of Rage action were Weatherman's "sectarianism, humorless franticness, their blind obedience to leadership,"

Police confront SDS
demonstrators at La Salle
and Madison, in Chicago's
Loop, during one of sev-
eral violent clashes in
October 1969. Photograph
reproduced courtesy of
UPI/Corbis-Bettmann.

and a misconception concerning the nature of adventurism.[31]

Another topic brought up in the leadership's self-criticism session concerned the effectiveness of a strategy of fighting with the police in the streets. According to Jeff Jones: "There was a position to the right of me which was, 'It was a failure. We shouldn't have done it.' And there was a position to the left of me, which was, 'It was a failure. We have to escalate.'"[32] It was suggested that confrontations with the police were bound to fail and should perhaps be replaced with some other tactic. The Tupamaro solution, named for the urban guerrillas then operating in Uruguay, was suggested. In practice, what this meant for Weather was to go underground and pick up the gun. After a long discussion, the Tupamaro solution was rejected for the time being, and instead, Weather again resolved to build "a strong presence on a national level, so as to compel every white youth to deal with the existence of a revolutionary white fighting force."[33] The arguments over tactics show that the radical New Left took itself, and the possibility of revolution in the US, very seriously at this point. As later developments would show, the arguments and ideas discussed by Weather in October 1969 would soon be the topic of many a leftist conversation throughout the country.

On Thursday afternoon, the 10th, the 2,500 National Guardsmen who had been on standby alert moved into the city. As a result, and because of the dwindling numbers of Weather people in the city, a major action planned for Friday was called off. It was to have been a "jailbreak" at local high schools. This tactic involved Weather members appearing en masse at a high school, distributing leaflets, chanting anti-war and revolutionary slogans, and urging the students to leave their classes. The Weather women, however, had proceeded with their plan to attack a draft board on Thursday morning. About seventy female activists gathered in Grant Park, where Bernardine Dohrn told them that "a few buck-shot wounds, a few pellets, mean we're doing the right thing here." Their fear, continued Dohrn, "has to be put up against the hunger, fear, death, and suffering of black, brown, and yellow people in this country and all over the world."[34] After Dohrn's pep talk, the women began marching toward the draft board a few blocks away. They were stopped by a police blockade and ordered to let go of their weapons, which included pieces of lead pipe and brick. Instead, the leaders of the march, including Dohrn, charged the police lines and were immediately attacked. After about twenty minutes of fighting between Weather and approximately 300 officers, the bruised and bloodied women were overwhelmed and placed in paddy wagons. None ever reached the draft board.

That afternoon, RYM II held a rally outside the courthouse where the Chicago 8 trial was taking place. The Chicago Panthers, the local chapter of the Young Lords, and some Weather members were also in attendance. The crowd num-bered around 2,500, not including more than 800 police officers. Because of the police presence and a threat from the sponsors of the rally, the Weather people in attendance did nothing, although their original plan was to invade the courthouse and disrupt the trial.

Before the final action on the Saturday, Weatherman was thrown out of the McCormick Seminary, one of the buildings it had been allowed to use as a movement center, after badly beating up an undercover policeman. A priest had walked in on the proceedings and, horrified at what he saw, gave Weather thirty minutes to leave. Not wishing to provoke the priest into calling the police, it complied. According to a Liberation News Service report the following week, police then raided another movement center and arrested forty protestors on a variety of felony charges, including attempted murder.[35]

The final action on Saturday began at noon on Haymarket square, where Weather had destroyed the commemorative police statue. Although only 20 or 30 people were present at the start, eventually close to 300 showed up. While demonstrators waited for the action to begin, plainclothes Chicago police officers arrested Mark Rudd, Jeff Jones, and two others on charges of assault, mob action, and resisting arrest, beating them badly in the process.

The march finally began around 1:30, an hour and a half later than scheduled. After short speeches by Weatherbureau members JJ and Dohrn, who argued that the Weather actions of the week would inspire activists even if they failed militarily, the marchers set off, proceeding in an orderly fashion for several blocks before rushing police lines. The fiercest fighting of the week took place over the next 30 or 40 minutes, before the police overpowered the Weather cadres. The number of casualties was great, considering the relatively small number of demonstrators. There were 110 arrests and many badly injured on both sides, including Richard Elrod, a Chicago corporate attorney who was originally thought to have been hit with a lead pipe on his spinal cord while he was pounding a demonstrator with his fists. Elrod was hospitalized with a broken neck, and a Weather man – Brian Flanagan – was charged with attempted murder. But, testimony at Flanagan's trial showed that Elrod had in fact accidentally hit his head against a wall while beating a protestor, and Flanagan was acquitted of the charge.[36] In contrast, the Saturday RYM II march and demonstration at a Caterpillar factory where workers were on strike attracted over 3,000 supporters and

Bernardine Dohrn and Brian Flanagan talk to supporters before entering the Criminal Courts building in Chicago on October 24, 1969. Hearings and trials were held that day for those arrested during the Chicago Loop riots of early October; Flanagan was accused of assailing chief city prosecutor Richard Elrod, Dohrn of being an SDS organizer. Photograph reproduced courtesy of UPI-Bettmann.

was welcomed by the residents of the inner-city neighborhood where it was held.

Most of the Weather people arrested were bailed out within a week by their families or friends. According to law-enforcement records, there were a total of 284 arrests, 40 of them on felony charges, and several serious injuries; bail charges exceeded $1.5 million. Of those arrested, 104 were college students, mostly from the Midwest and New York. Another 20 were high-school students, and the rest were either part-time or full-time activists. Fifty-seven police were hospitalized and over one million dollars of damage was caused to property in the city of Chicago.[37]

NOTES

1. SDS National Council, "Bring the War Home," *New Left Notes*, July 23, 1969.

2. Mike Klonsky, "Why I Quit," *New Left Notes*, August 29, 1969.

3. Terry Robbins and Mark Rudd, "Goodbye Mike," *New Left Notes*, August 29, 1969.

4. Klonsky, "Why I Quit."

5. Tom Hayden, *The Trial*, Holt, Rinehart & Winston, New York, 1970, p. 29.

6. Armando, "Electric Mud," *Chicago Seed*, 4: 5, (August 1969).

7. Mark Kramer, "Rock Imperialists," *New Left Notes*, August 8, 1969.

8. Cathy Wilkerson, quoted in Ronald Fraser, *1968: A Student Generation in Revolt*, Pantheon, New York, 1988, p. 312.

9. "Bring the War Home," *New Left Notes*, July 23, 1969.

10. Ibid.

11. Ibid.

12. *The Fire Next Time* (*New Left Notes*), September 20, 1969.

13. *New Left Notes*, August 1, 1969.

14. From conversation with George Katsiaficas, December 1989.

15. SDS, "Weatherman vs. The Pigs," leaflet, *Students for a Democratic Society Papers*, 1958–70, Microfilming Corporation of America, Glen Rock, N.J., 1958, 1970, Reel 41.

16. *FIRE!*, September 20, 1969.

17. Ibid.

18. Larry Grathwohl, *Bringing Down America: An FBI Informer with the Weathermen*, Arlington House, New Rochelle, N.Y., 1976.

19. "Towards a Women's Militia," *New Left Notes*, September 12, 1969.

20. Weatherman leaflet, Fall 1969.

21. Much of the information for this chapter was drawn from the Weatherman paper *FIRE!*; an article by the Weather man Shin'ya Ono which appeared in the December 1969 *Leviathan* (San Francisco, 1969); an article by Andrew Kopkind in the magazine *Hard Times* (New Weekly Project, Washington, D.C., October 20, 1969); Tom Thomas's *The Second Battle of Chicago: Chicago, 1969*, SDS, Grinnell, Iowa, 1969; and conversations with three people who participated in the Days of Rage, all of whom wish to remain anonymous. I have not noted all my sources within the text, only the actual quotes from these readings.

22. Quoted in *Black Panther*, October 18, 1969.

23. Editors, *Chicago Seed*, 4: 7 (October 1969).

24. Bill Ayers, "A Strategy to Win," *New Left Notes*, September 12, 1969.

25. Staff, "Don't Mourn, Organize," *Old Mole*, September 14, 1969.

26. Carl Davidson and Randy Furst "Weatherman Goes It Alone in Kick-Ass Brawl," *Guardian*, October 18, 1969.

27. Liberation News Service (LNS), *Dock of the Bay*, San Francisco, November 1969, p. 1.

28. Susan Stern, *With the Weatherman*, Doubleday, Garden City, N.Y., 1975, p. 134.

29. Shin'ya Ono, from *Leviathan*, p. 256.

30. From conversation with Steve, December 1989.

31. Shin'ya Ono, from *Leviathan*, p. 260.

32. Jeff Jones quoted in Joan Morrison and Robert K. Morrison, *From Camelot to Kent State: The Sixties Experience in the Words of Those Who Lived It*, Times Books, New York, 1987, p. 314.

33. Ibid., p. 261.

34. LNS, *Dock of the Bay*, p. 11.

35. Ibid.

36. Kirkpatrick, Sale, *SDS*, Vintage, New York, p. 611.

37. Subcommittee to Investigate the Administration of the Internal Security Act, Committee on the Judiciary, US Congress *Extent of Subversion in the New Left*, March 1970, Government Printing Office, Washington D.C., 1970, pp. 443–8.

4...

Down the Tunnel: Going Underground

Within days of the final action in Chicago on Saturday, October 11 the Weatherbureau was claiming a victory. According to Shin'ya Ono, Weather regarded the week of actions as successful for three reasons.[1] First, the willingness of Weather people to lay their lives on the line would push other white radicals to make a similar commitment. This view was based naively on the belief that the media coverage of the Days of Rage had created an image of strength for the watching world, much like the Tet offensive of the National Liberation Front in 1968. Bernardine Dohrn later remarked, "We were determined to carry out an action that would reveal how passionately we felt and that we were on the other side."[2]

The development of cadre which occurred in Chicago was another element of Weather's perceived victory. Prior to the Days of Rage, it had developed a fairly tight and mobile force which was honed by the experiences gained in Chicago. While not without its individual differences, the group impressed the rest of the New Left with its ability to act in a concerted way.

The third aspect of Weather's assessment concerned material damage. Its stated aims had included the destruction of property and fighting the police, criteria that the four days in Chicago certainly met. But despite these claims to victory Weatherman believed that the increased repression that was sure to follow, as well as the injuries sustained by the street fighters, suggested that mass street actions, while necessary, were a losing tactic.

Favorable commentary on the Days of Rage came from non-Weatherman sources as well. Andrew Kopkind, who co-edited the New Left weekly *Hard Times* and took part in the Chicago action, echoed Weatherman's assessment of its commitment when he stated that it "challenges the validity of the intellectual left, which functions as a comfortable culture of opposition; instead, it asks that radicals become revolutionaries, completely collectivize their lives, and struggle to the death." Later in the same article Kopkind addressed Weather's mistakes. He attributed these to a "simple-mindedness about the varieties of political experience in America" and to a fascination with violence. Kopkind, who had shared a jail cell with Weather men arrested in the Saturday march, ended his article with the observation that in modern America "simply not to fear fighting is a kind of winning."[3]

Dissenting from the mainstream Panther line, Eldridge Cleaver wrote a letter to blacks from exile in Algeria in support of Weather, asking, "Did we ever pay attention to white radicals when they told us to keep our shoot-outs clean and middle-class orderly?" He also supported Weather's call for the overthrow of the United States through violent revolution: "In times of revolution . . . I love the angels of destruction as opposed to the devils . . . of law and order."[4] The rest of the Panthers, who were based in Oakland, California, under Huey Newton's leadership, criticized Cleaver's and Weatherman's approach to revolution in the United States. These Panthers held the opinion that "black revolutionaries had to set an example," not by either adopting electoral politics or immediately picking up the gun and going underground, but by doing whatever it took to maintain a revolutionary profile and to educate as many people as they could before the state "drove them underground."[5] It wasn't that Newton and his followers objected to armed struggle, but their opinion of the situation in the US in autumn 1969 held that until large numbers of people supported the revolution, the repression which followed any army confrontation could only isolate the revolutionary forces and destroy the hope of revolution. The Panther forces represented by Cleaver, on the other hand, like Weatherman, believed they already had enough support and that the time had come for revolution.

Not all the commentary on the Days of Rage was favorable, of course. Much white radical activity did now become more confrontational, in part because of the example of the Days of Rage, but just as much in reaction to the repressive measures against the movement by the state. The leap toward revolution that many white New Leftists took in late 1969 was similar to their leap into massive resistance in 1968, and was attributable to no particular group or party, but stemmed from a general sense that the stakes needed to be raised if the war in Vietnam and against the black people in America was to be stopped. Weatherman did not now attract a rush of recruits.

The prevalent definition of revolution within the

movement in 1969 was the espousal of the destruction of the imperialist system in the United States and its replacement by some form of socialism. The word "revolution" was often used to describe tactics which went beyond defensive action and took an offensive line in the form of street fighting or bombings. For Weatherman, revolution meant to fight in support of wars of national liberation in the third world and to eventually install a socialist government in the US in support of third-world revolutions. Most other groups defined revolution somewhat differently: the Panthers desired self-determination for America's black population, for example, and the Yippies wanted an America characterized by the culture of youth rebellion.

For all those in the New Left who saw revolution as the solution, the question of violence was the foremost issue. Given the pacifist past of many groups and individuals, it was not easy for them to rationalize violence as a strategy and consequently most opted for it only in response to attack. Weather, on the other hand, had fewer qualms and was convinced that planned offensive actions were necessary because what was at stake was no longer proving that it was on the right side, but seizing military power. The state would only be overcome when it no longer had a monopoly on such power. This thinking was basic to Weather's strategy in Chicago and would remain so, with differences developing only in tactics.

Those radicals who differed from Weather in its definition of revolution criticized both its theory and its tactics. According to Tom Hayden, among others, Weather's ideological stance prevented its members from being "guerrillas swimming like fish among the people" and, instead, made them "more like commandos, fifth columnists, operating behind enemy lines" in support of third-world revolutionaries.

Hayden insisted that the American revolution needed to be more than a movement in support of others because, "as misfits of dying capitalism," youth and other disempowered whites also had to revolt in order to preserve their way of life.[6] Stew Albert, a longtime activist and Yippie, concurred, remarking that although the youth movement needed to wholeheartedly support the national liberation struggles of the world he, for one, "wasn't organizing a movement around suffering – of Vietnamese, blacks, or anyone, but presumably one to end suffering."[7]

From the Yippies' vantage point, the idea of setting a date for a battle with the state was ridiculous: it provided the police with a greater capacity to counter-attack, and it also took away the element of surprise, the activists' only advantage. In addition, the Yippies argued, given the movement's anti-hierarchical nature, its non-structure, and the resultant fluctuations in commitment and strength, planned attacks were inappropriate.

Pointing out the differences between the planned, offensive violence of Weatherman and Yippie's spontaneous, defensive version, Abbie Hoffman termed Weatherman's confrontations "Gandhian violence for the element of purging guilt through moral witness."[8] Ironically, it was the complaint of many of the founders of Weatherman that actions stemming from moral witness were not enough in the current conjuncture.

The harshest criticism of Weatherman in the revolutionary New Left came from the *Guardian* collective. In their report on the Days of Rage, Carl Davidson and Randy Furst called the action a "fiasco" controlled by the police with "brutal precision."[9] The *Guardian*'s politics were closer then to RYM II, and the remainder of the issue detailed its actions that same week, praising its attempts to link up with workers ready to strike at an International Harvester plant (provoking a walk-out) and with lower-paid workers at a Chicago hospital. The *Guardian* lamented the relatively small numbers drawn by both RYM II and Weatherman, and even though commentary was more favorable to the former, the articles about the Weatherman action at least treated the organization seriously – something Weather did not reciprocate when speaking publicly about RYM II.

The *Guardian* criticized Weatherman for its distrust of American workers and for placing them in the same camp as the military and the rest of the ruling class. Like others had before, the *Guardian* reminded Weather that nothing was as important as revolutionary work among the people, especially youth. Davidson and Furst also argued that the Weatherman-organized "surrealist contretemps" of the Days of Rage gave the moderate New Left and its liberal sympathizers a perfect reason not to adopt and promote revolutionary politics.[10] It was Furst and Davidson's contention that people risked participation in actions like those staged by Weatherman in Chicago only when they perceived a threat to their self-interest, as did the Vietnamese or the American blacks. By not seriously recognizing the oppression of other US workers, youth, and women, and organizing them around their specific oppressions, Weatherman, it was argued, insured its limited appeal.

Much of RYM II's criticism of Weatherman centred on their different perceptions of the role of the youth movement. Yippies and many other leftist groups had begun to organize youth solely on the basis of their oppression as youth. Weatherman also believed that, because of the war and the draft, and the burgeoning counter-culture, youth was

Cover of *Class War comix*, fall 1969. A *FIRE!* publication, from the author's private collection.

either a class unto itself or "an embryonic part of a larger movement that reflect[ed] the transformation of the nineteenth century working class into a new working class."[11] Yippies and others organized primarily around this age-specific oppression, while Weatherman attempted to direct youth's anger into fighting for the revolutions of the third world, and RYM II and other Marxist-Leninist and Maoist-leaning groups saw youth mostly as a way to reach US workers. All these organizations hoped to transform the rebellious nature of the counter-culture into an anti-imperialist revolutionary movement, but RYM II hoped to ignite the older workers with the spark of youth, while the Yippies and Weather preferred to forgo the support of older workers and fight the revolution without them.

• • •

To anyone who wasn't there, it is difficult to comprehend the extent of the fear and suspicion in the New Left and counter-culture during the late 1960s to mid-1970s. Most of it was well founded. Black, Native American, and Chicano activists were gunned down, white activists were railroaded on questionable or fabricated charges, ordinary young people and students were beaten and arrested merely for protesting or because of their appearance.

After the Days of Rage action Weather was the subject of at least two federal investigations. According to Larry Grathwohl, who worked underground in Weather from early fall in 1969 until the summer of 1970, the FBI opened a file on the group in late October 1969. At around the same time the Senate Committee of Internal Security opened an investigation as well. Both investigations were driven by the belief that Weatherman constituted a major threat to the internal security of the United States and that it was controlled at least partially by foreign governments. These investigations were part of a counter-intelligence operation against the whole of the New Left known as the Counter Intelligence Program (COINTELPRO). Frank Donner, author of several books on the US government's attacks on dissent, described this operation as "an undisguised assault by the self-appointed defenders of the American way of life."[12]

As far as Weather was concerned, the primary objective of police agencies was to stop its activities and arrest its members. Before the group went underground, this objective was achieved by police spies and informants at meetings and demonstrations and by perpetual harassment and arrests on contrived charges. Michael P. Wood, a Weather friend, wrote an article for *Win* magazine detailing his experiences in one week of hanging out at a Boston Weather collective in November 1969. He tells how police followed members on their daily rounds and of his own arrest on a fictitious (or John Doe) warrant at a picket line outside a courthouse. Some Weather members were on trial for an earlier action at Harvard University's Center for International Affairs, when the director of the Center was attacked and his office vandalized. The trial ended in heavy fines for four people and three one-year sentences for Eric Mann – sentences much greater than those given to others arrested on the same charges in a non-political context. After a weekend away from Boston, Wood returned to stand trial. The action at Harvard for which he was arrested occurred while he was working on Long Island, but despite this fact and undisputed alibis presented by his lawyers, Wood was convicted. As he wrote, "I was convicted and am now out on appeal. For what – associating with

Weatherman or looking like them? Imagine what the Panthers are up against!"[13]

• • •

A nationwide General Electric strike in November provided many white radicals with an opportunity to express their solidarity with workers. Most leftists saw the strike as a chance to create new alliances and expand the movement beyond its student base. Weatherman, however, showed up at picket lines and demonstrations called to support the strike with signs and literature labeling the General Electric workers as pigs. A participant in the strike in the Boston area told of a Weather sign stating something along the lines of "Ho Ho Chi Minh, the NLF are gonna kill GE workers."[14]

Preferring to organize youth, when they did any organizing at all, Weatherman distributed its newspaper *FIRE!* on college and high-school campuses, and at other places where young people gathered, such as rock concerts. The paper was full of rhetoric and graphics reflecting the organization's decision to "fight in a public way, not a covert way." In an attack on mainstream anti-war organizations (the National Mobilization to End the War in Vietnam, or Mobe, and the Moratorium Committee) mobilizing for the November 15 Mobilization to End the War in Vietnam, Weatherman labeled legal demonstrations as pointless in the United States because it was fundamentally anti-democratic. *FIRE!* blamed the leadership of the anti-war movement for its failure to grow politically and tactically – a criticism which overlooked the SDS's earlier failure to organize a national anti-war movement.[15]

FIRE! did, however, praise the upswing in attacks on the state – "200 ROTC buildings trashed, hundreds of walkouts

Cartoon illustrating Weatherman's experience at the "Mobilization to end the war in Vietnam" demonstration in Washington, DC, November 15, 1969. A *FIRE!* publication, from the author's private collection.

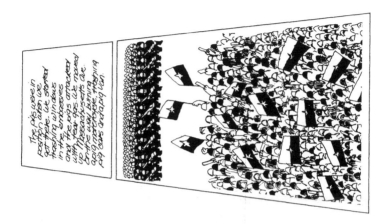

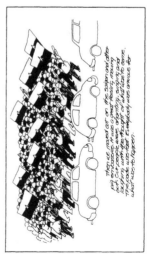

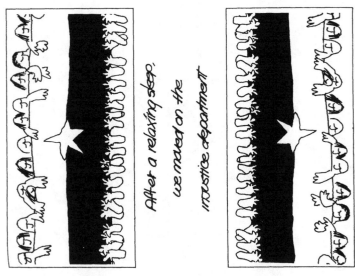

Diana Oughton (right, in beret) arrives at an SDS convention at Flint, Michigan, on December 27, 1969. The photograph, one of the last ever of Oughton, was taken by Flint police who watched the meeting closely. Photograph reproduced courtesy of UPI-Bettmann.

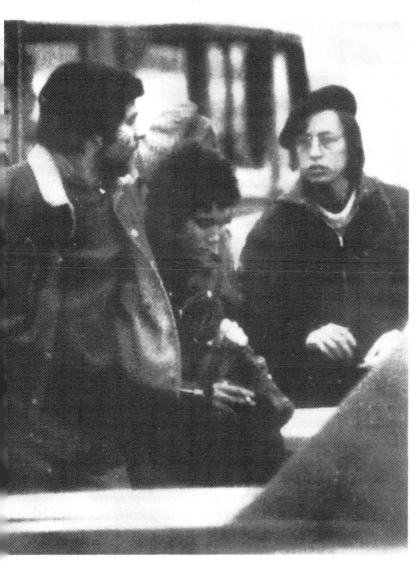

and fires at high schools, and many street actions" – and called on anti-war demonstrators to increase material attacks on the state's power. Referring specifically to the upcoming demonstration in Washington, D.C., on November 15, Weatherman urged its members to raise the level of confrontation: "It is neither numbers nor loud voices alone that will bring imperialism down, but real material attacks on the state."[16]

Boston Weather members took this to heart when they shot out some windows at the Cambridge police station on November 8, according to the questionable testimony of a 16-year-old boy who was living at the Weather collective's house at the time and had allegedly been beaten by the police after his arrest on charges stemming from an argument with a store owner. Some twenty-three Weather members were arrested and charged with conspiracy to commit murder and promote anarchy.[17]

Three days before the November 15 Mobilization to End the War a series of bombs exploded in the offices of Chase Manhattan, Standard Oil, and General Motors in New York. The bombings were not Weatherman actions, but they were applauded by the organization as further evidence of the growing militancy of the New Left, and, by some individuals, as a welcome contrast to the increasing legitimacy of the mainstream anti-war movement. In addition, the formation of hundreds of local anti-war and anti-imperialist committees and coalitions separate from the national organizations was taken as further proof by Weather of the growth in revolutionary consciousness in the United States. A rally at the South Vietnamese embassy in Washington, D.C. on November 14, called by an alliance of anti-imperialist organizations, further enhanced this perception; over 10,000 demonstrators fought pitched battles with the police for several hours.[18]

Although much of the corporate media and many liberal politicians did their best to portray the November 15 Mobilization to End the War as just another exercise in free speech, the growing numbers of anti-imperialist activists were determined to push the action beyond those limits. The conspiracy trial of the Chicago 8 provided them with a perfect foil. On the afternoon of November 15, Yippies, Weather members, and thousands of others left the main rally on the Capitol mall and chanting "Stop the Trial" marched on the Justice Department building. Augmenting the chant with "Free Bobby Seale, Free Kim Agnew" (in reference to Black Panther and the Vice-President's 14-year-old daughter who, it was rumored, had been forbidden to wear a black armband in solidarity with the demonstrators), more than 20,000 demonstrators surrounded the building. A game of push and shove with the law went on for about twenty minutes until a Yippie activist replaced the US flag on the flagpole in front of the building with an NLF banner. "The pigs understood the insult," reported the *Quicksilver Times*, "and were up for the challenge. A skirmish and brief tug of war ensued with the different flags alternately being raised and lowered."[19] Eventually the police attacked, throwing tear gas and assaulting the crowd. The fighting continued until midnight.

The size and militancy of the crowds at both the Justice Department demonstration and the night before at the South Vietnamese embassy stirred hopes in the New Left of building a broad-based nationwide revolutionary youth movement. Weatherman too was excited and began to organize for its next conference, billed as a war council, where such a movement would be forged.

● ● ●

On December 4, Chicago police raided the apartment of Black Panthers Mark Clark and Fred Hampton and killed them in cold blood. These murders chilled the entire revolutionary movement. A cry for revenge went up throughout the New Left, especially from Weatherman. In the streets, however, action was limited to a few rallies, some fire bombings, and leafletting. Weather people did nothing other than join a couple of marches and firebomb some police cars; their relative inactivity reflected the organization's internal doubts about the efficacy of street actions and, at the same time, its inability then to carry out armed attacks. Later they were to see their inertia at this time as defeatist.

> In white Amerika, we too understand that we can regain our lives only through struggle . . . The meeting will be a gathering of the tribes – a war council. Only with each other can we figure out how to build the kind of organization that can lead us toward victory – toward the smashing of U.S. imperialism . . . We have to learn from one another . . . We are going to learn to work and struggle with each other in order to change ourselves and each other into revolutionaries . . . It's going to be different . . . It's going to be out of sight.
>
> Letter to white radicals from Weatherman, December 1969[20]

One of the first things those who attended the war council noticed as they entered the run-down ballroom in Flint, Michigan on December 2, 1969 was the freshly dried blood in the corner. The result of a knife fight between locals at a dance the night before the council convened, the blood symbolized the bloodlust at the council that many of those present would speak of later.

If the blood didn't catch the eye, then perhaps the giant cardboard machine gun suspended from the ceiling did. The gun was of course symbolic of the direction Weather planned to take, although almost everyone else in attendance – some White Panthers, Yippies, independent activists, and members of the underground media – questioned the practicality of such a move. The Weatherbureau was convinced, and the council was intended to persuade the rest.

After an opening speech by Mark Rudd in which he compared himself to Captain Ahab in *Moby Dick* – "I'm monomaniacal like Captain Ahab. He was possessed by one thought: destroying the great white whale. We should be like Captain Ahab and possess one thought – destruction of the mother country" – the days were marked by earnest discussions around various points raised by the Weather line.[21] Some discussions concerned the necessity for immediate armed violence, others the targets of that violence. Perhaps to prove the sincerity of their "commitment to" total revolution, some Weather members discussed the political correctness of the murder of white babies. Another discussion dealing only with theory was limited to women. Organized by committed Weather women ever more intent on establishing their identity within the organization, the conversation centered on male-chauvinist perceptions of women among both genders, and how those perceptions held back all Weather people from making revolution.

Weather had invited young counter-cultural radicals to come to Flint and rebuild "SDS as a forum for the ideological struggle." With respect to the fleeting victories of the past, the leadership suggested that their temporary nature came "from a fundamental misunderstanding of power." The Weatherbureau's solution was to target sites of power and to attack them as if fighting "part of the international war."[22] If that wasn't possible, then chaos in the streets was seen as the next best option. In the words of one leaflet, "The future of our struggle is the future of crime in the streets."[23] Although Weatherman's stated intention preceding the council was to build a broad-based anti-imperialist revolutionary movement, its politics and its unwillingness to fit them to the larger concerns of counter-cultural youth made such a goal unobtainable. For those not in Weather, disagreeing with what the Weatherbureau said proved virtually impossible, despite the implications of the open invitation promising a revolutionary and counter-cultural "gathering of the tribes." If a dissenter wasn't shouted down, his/her argument would be lost in a flood of "rhetoric that never addressed itself to the point." According to another observer: "It wasn't a gathering of tribes, they [Weather] just talked to each other."[24]

Despite all its stated pre-council intentions to continue its confrontational street-fighting tactics, no matter what the cost, by the end of the council, the Weatherbureau had opted to go underground. It was not an easily made decision for most, and it would intensify the process of isolation Weatherman had begun in June.

Weather's decision to move underground and engage in armed struggle was propelled by its understanding of repression in the United States in 1969. Linda Evans stated in an interview from prison in 1991 that she decided to go underground and "participate in armed struggle because of the rage [she] felt after the FBI/police raids on Black Panther Party offices and homes all over the US and particularly the murder of Fred Hampton and Mark Clark by Chicago police."[25] It was this rage, coupled with frustration at failing to draw large numbers to Chicago, that was a driving force in the

Weatherbureau's decision. The Chicago failure also led Weather to conclude, at least for the moment, that because white radicals were unwilling to follow its program a race war was inevitable. For its part, Weatherman wanted to be on the side of the blacks.

Weatherman had given up on white people and saw the organization's role solely as one of causing chaos in support of the blacks and other national liberation movements, in the style of the abolitionist John Brown. Although some members, among them Jim Mellen , still believed it was possible to organize American working-class youth into a revolutionary movement and disagreed with the decision to go underground, their dissension fell on deaf ears. It was apparent to most attendants that the decision had been made before the council began, even though the stated aim of the meeting was to rebuild SDS. According to Susan Stern, members were told of the decision only after a closed-door meeting of the leadership. The announcement was followed by a speech from Dohrn extolling the Tate–LaBianca murders in Los Angeles the previous August – murders Charles Manson and his followers were eventually convicted of. "Manson," said Dohrn, "killed those pigs, then they ate dinner in the same room with them, then they shoved a fork into a victim's stomach!" She continued, "Parents are now gonna' tell their kids to stay away from home vacation – they're afraid they'll get offed in their sleep." The speech was later criticized by most listeners, including Dohrn, but not much was said at the time.[26] Susan Stern called Dohrn's commendation of the Manson family's actions "the last putrid drop of American poison" in Weatherman and believed that they represented the despair felt by the New Left's most dedicated adherents.[27]

After the days of discussion members spent the nights partying. They danced and sang, and there was a good deal of free-for-all sexual activity as well. As far as drug-taking went, though, both Weather and non-Weather sources agreed that it was to be discreet and minimal so that police could not use it as a pretext for breaking up the meeting. The celebration seemed contrived to many observers, as did Weather members' donning of beads and sandals. It took more than beads, rock-and-roll, and drugs to be part of the counter-cultural revolution. Weatherman's objectification of youth led them to objectify its culture too. Tibor Kalman of the *Rat* commented: "Weatherman attempt[ed] to suck off the youth culture in a way that's not qualitatively different from the Bill Grahams and the Woodstock moneyfuckers."[28]

All in all, despite the preceding rhetoric, the war council achieved only a consolidation of the Weatherman hierarchy and analysis, and a decision to go underground – the logical conclusion of the organization's distrust of its own potential base of support. In the months to come, America would become more aware of Weather than ever before because of its armed propaganda, but its failure to hook up with other white revolutionary groups at the council was unfortunate. When Weather went underground, "some of the best minds in the movement" went too.[29]

NOTES

1. In *Leviathan*, December 1969.
2. *Underground*, directed by Emile DeAntonio, with Mary Wexler and members of Weather Underground Organization, First Run Features, New York, 1976.
3. *Hard Times*, October 20, 1969.
4. Eldridge Cleaver, "On the Weatherman," *Berkeley Tribe*, November 13, 1969.
5. Huey Newton, from "Huey Newton Talks to the Movement about the

Black Panther Party, Cultural Nationalism, SNCC, Liberals and White Revolutionaries," in *The Black Panthers Speak*, ed. Philip S. Foner, J.A. Lippincott, Philadelphia, 1970, pp. 63–6.

6. Hayden, *The Trial*, Holt, Rinehart & Winston, New York, 1970, p. 94.
7. Stew Albert et al., "Radical RapUp," *Berkeley Tribe*, October 31, 1969.
8. Ibid.
9. Carl Davidson and Randy Furst, "Hurricane or Hot Air," *Guardian*, October 18, 1969.
10. Ibid.
11. From the introduction to H. Gintis, "The New Working Class and Revolutionary Youth," *Socialist Revolution*, May–June 1970, Agenda Publishing, San Francisco. The article discusses the role of student rebellions in advance capitalist societies. Gintis's basic thesis is: since the role of education is to train students to perform tasks demanded by the new capitalist technology, disruption of the educational process strikes a blow against the established order and furthers the development of working-class consciousness.
12. Frank Donner, *The Age of Surveillance*, Alfred Knopf, New York, 1980, p. 232.
13. Michael P. Wood, "Weather Report: A Dove in the Kitchen," *Win*, New York, February 1, 1970, p. 7.
14. From conversation with Pete Bohmer, fall 1989.
15. *FIRE!*, November 7, 1969.
16. Ibid.
17. Staff, "Repression Hits Weatherman", *Old Mole*, Boston, December 4, 1969.
18. "Injustice Dept. March," *Quicksilver Times*, November 1969.
19. Ibid.
20. Liberation News Service, Washington, D.C., December 1969.
21. Ken Kelley and David Schanoes, "Moby Dick," *Ann Arbor Argus*, December 31, 1970.
22. *FIRE!*, December 6, 1969.
23. From a packet distributed at the war council in Flint, Michigan, December 1969.
24. Terry Brecker, *Quicksilver Times*, January 9, 1970.
25. "Interview with Linda Evans, Laura Whitehorn, and Susan Rosenberg," in Queers United in Support of Political Prisoners, "Arm the Spirit," 1991: http.//burn. ucsd. edu/~ats.
26. "Moby Dick," *Ann Arbor Argus*, December 31, 1970.
27. Susan Stern, *With the Weatherman*, Doubleday, Garden City, N.Y., 1975, p. 205.
28. Tibor Kalman, "Homemade Weather Guide," *Rat*, New York, January 1970.
29. *Quicksilver Times*, January 9, 1970.

5...

Women, the Counter-culture, and the Weather People

Women are something else. This time, we're going to kick out all the jams, and the boys will just have to hustle to keep up, or else drop out and openly join the power structure of which they are already the illegitimate sons. Any man who claims he is serious about wanting to divest himself of cock privileges should trip on this: all male leadership out of the Left is the only way; and it's going to happen, whether through men stepping down or through women seizing the helm. It's up to the "brothers" – after all, sexism is their concern, not ours; we're too busy getting ourselves together to deal with their bigotry.

Robin Morgan[1]

In the February 6, 1970, all-women's issue of *Rat*, a New York based underground paper, former SDS member Robin Morgan exposed the "liberal cooptative masks on the face of sexist hate and fear" and demanded that both women and men in the movement rethink their position on the role of women in history and in the present. She insisted that men were the enemy of women and accused New Left organizations of not being truly revolutionary because of their refusal to seriously address this question. According to Morgan, women were the real Left because of their experience of gender oppression which, along with racism, predated capitalism. The Left functioned "as a microcosm of the capitalist economy, with men competing for power and status at the top, and women doing all the work at the bottom." The women's collective at *Rat* warned men throughout the Left from the Mobe to the Panthers, to RYM II, to counter-culture radicals, and to Weatherman, that women were "rising with a fury older and potentially greater than any force in history, and this time we will be free or no one will survive."[2]

In Morgan's letter, Weather women were equated with the "Manson slaves," and the "Stanley Kowalski image and . . . practice of sex on demand for males" in Weatherman was sharply criticized. Furthermore, the Weather women's adoption of the group's macho style was not revolutionary or liberating, but merely a "last desperate grab at male approval." Robin Morgan was not alone in her criticism of Weatherman's male chauvinism. Bread and Roses, a women's collective from the Boston area, expressed their anger over the group's male bias: "The machismo and militarism characterizing Weatherman actions do not merely reflect tactical errors or improper application of theory. Indeed, their male chauvinism stems from a basic misunderstanding of the nature of women's oppression." Like other groups on the revolutionary New Left, Bread and Roses challenged the Weather idea that struggles for equal rights in the context of imperialism were a racist tactic and argued that the issues of women's rights, youth culture, and workers' oppression could beget revolutionary struggles if analyzed in a revolutionary framework.

Furthermore, with regard to Weatherman's internal dialectic, Bread and Roses claimed that its desire to destroy monogamy was based on an objectification of women and relationships, as well as an oversimplified analysis of the role of monogamy in women's lives under monopoly capitalism. According to the feminist collective, monogamous relationships and, consequently, the nuclear family were necessities for most women given the limited economic and social structures available to them in US society. Until true economic equality existed for all women, regardless of class or color, the security, however precarious, afforded by monogamy would insure its continued practicality and popularity. Bread and Roses did not defend the proliferation of exclusive couplings, but tried to explain their existence politically.

Finally, Bread and Roses stated that Weatherman's methods in its campaign to smash monogamy might "produce effectiveness and homogeneity and loyalty – but it doesn't produce freedom." In addition, it only truly freed men from responsibility and, consequently, replicated the structures already in existence.[3]

In the same issue of *Rat*, an article by a Weather woman accused women's separatist organizations of falling short in their theory by mistakenly blaming men for gender oppression rather than US imperialism. "Women," wrote the Weather woman, "needed to learn how to build this new society where people don't destroy one another but build each other." She admitted that it was sometimes hard to work with men but "there was no other way to make the revolution." As if in answer to Morgan's comparison of Weather women with Manson's sex slaves, the writer described the Weather campaign against monogamy and the resultant sexual experimentation as "creating new standards for men and women to relate to" according to which making revolution became the common denominator.[4]

The struggles in the New Left over the women question were instructive to Weather in the long run. The organization, which had always been extremely intolerant of oppressive attitudes, now found its male members attacked for sexism. The arguments which occurred could have torn Weather apart but, instead, created a dynamic which provided lessons for all of its organizational work. The men's realization that they, too, were capable of counter-revolutionary thought and action allowed them to see that most prejudices resulted from ignorance. This realization paved the way for a new approach to inter-organizational relationships. By trying to work out their own shortcomings while maintaining a revolutionary perspective, they were forced to acknowledge that individuals were capable of change, whatever their previous prejudices.

● ● ●

The move underground continued at a rapid pace. Individuals wrestled with the implications of the move and decided whether they were willing to sever all ties with their families and friends. Weatherbureau members met with local collectives and, after serious criticism sessions, issued directives about who would stay and who would be asked to leave.

Those who weren't willing to leave when asked to were unceremoniously kicked out. The techniques during the criticism sessions were similar to those used in the summer and fall, only now virtually all of them involved the use of LSD. This was considered an ideal way to ferret out any police agents since it would be difficult for anyone, especially an informer, to maintain his/her cover while under the influence of LSD. It was not foolproof, however, as the informer Larry Grathwohl related in his book. He was able to fake swallowing a tablet of LSD and ended up being asked to join an elite group of Weather which was sent to Detroit.

By February 1970, all of those who remained in Weatherman had gone underground. Members spent time in city halls searching for the false identifications they would need to apply for public assistance or social-security numbers. Many of those who had access to trust funds or bank accounts liquidated them and pooled the money with that of the other underground cells. Any property of value, like televisions or stereos, was sold, and that money too was pooled. The national offices let their utility bills go unpaid, and on February 9, 1970 the last open SDS office in Chicago was quietly vacated. A call had been made on the 8th to Vicky Grabiner, a sympathetic employee of the State Historical Society of Wisconsin – where a large collection of Left documents are stored – inquiring if they were interested in the SDS archive. Grabiner obtained $300 and bought the contents of the office. While she was loading the documents into her van in the early morning of February 9, a police car left its surveillance post nearby and officers tried unsuccessfully to seize the materials.[5]

Some Weather people participated in nationwide The Day After (TDA) protests against the convictions of the Chicago defendants (now numbering 7 rather than 8, as Bobby Seale had been removed from the docket) in February, but most of the better-known members chose to remain hidden, applauding the youth insurrections from their underground vantage point. Local collectives in specific towns and cities no longer existed. Instead, members organized themselves into cells of 3, 4 or 5 people and spread out across the country, with most of the cells located on the coasts. Of the several hundred members who had participated in the Days of Rage, only a couple of hundred remained. Communication between the cells was dependent on sympathetic aboveground supporters (some of whom were Weather members who did not wish to go underground). Meetings were arranged secretly with the use of code words and names, and mailboxes registered under false names. Each cell was committed to armed action and was instructed by the Weatherbureau to come up with a list of potential targets. The list was relayed verbally to the Weatherbureau which would discuss the merits and disadvantages of each target. Little was committed to paper since anything written down was potentially incriminating evidence should the police discover the location of a Weather house. Due to the decentralized structure of the organization, it was rare for one cell to know of another's plans.

It was for precisely this reason that Weather members around the nation were shocked when they heard news on March 7 of an explosion in New York City which had killed at least one of their comrades. Diana Oughton, Kathy Boudin, Cathy Wilkerson, Ted Gold, and Terry Robbins had been living and building bombs in Wilkerson's parents' Greenwich Village townhouse on West 11th Street. The bombs they were making, composed of nails wrapped around an explosive center that would spray shrapnel when exploded, were

The bombed-out town-
house in Greenwich
Village's West 11th Street
in which Diana Oughton,
Ted Gold, and Terry
Robbins died. Photograph
reproduced courtesy of
UPI-Bettmann.

designed to kill. Two weeks prior to the accidental explosion at the townhouse, this Weather cell had firebombed the home of Justice Murtagh, the judge presiding over the trial of Panther 21, Black Panthers from the New York branch who had been indicted by a grand jury on charges of conspiring to bomb police stations, Macy's, the Bronx Botanical Gardens, and government buildings around the city. Despite the amount of media attention generated by the firebombing, some members of the cell felt it had not been a success because it had failed to cause sufficient material damage. These members, purported to be Terry Robbins and Ted Gold, had devised a campaign which Bernardine Dohrn would later describe as a "large-scale, almost random bombing offensive," including an attack on a dance for military officers.[6] Although discussions were continuing within the cell over the merits of the plan – with some members still unsure – a wiring mistake made during the bomb-building on the morning of March 6 killed three Weather members and destroyed Wilkerson's parents' house.

The two survivors – Cathy Wilkerson and Kathy Boudin – half-naked and dazed from the explosion, fled the building. Ann Hoffman, wife of actor Dustin Hoffman, who lived next door, took the two women into her house and helped them clean up. Another neighbor gave them some clothes to wear. By the time fire and police units arrived on the scene, Boudin and Wilkerson were gone, and before police detectives figured out that the explosion was caused by a bomb and not escaping gas, as was first believed, the entire Weather organization had gone underground.

Once the fire was out, police and arson investigators began searching through the debris for victims. The first body they found was that of Ted Gold. He had been crushed by a beam moments after the explosion. The bodies of the other victims were virtually destroyed. It wasn't until police found part of his thumb several weeks later (and after Weather commemorated his death in a communiqué) that they were able to positively identify Terry Robbins. The third victim, Diana Oughton, was not identified for ten days. Police did find other evidence, however: four cartons of explosives containing 57 sticks of dynamite, 30 blasting caps, and some clocks in the process of being converted into timing devices.

• • •

The deaths of the three Weather people, all founder members of the organization, created its first martyrs and brought the newly underground organization abruptly into public view.

Oughton, the daughter of a wealthy Illinois businessman, had worked in government poverty programs during her college years and then run a community school for poor children with her lover, Bill Ayers. The continuing war in Vietnam had forced both Oughton and Ayers to look for more radical solutions to fundamental social problems. The two joined SDS in early 1968 and were instrumental in building one of the organization's most influential chapters at Ann Arbor, a group that was essential to the founding of Weatherman.

Ted Gold joined Columbia SDS in 1967 out of his frustration with the growing US involvement in Vietnam and the worsening living conditions of the residents of Harlem. He was a key organizer of a fall 1967 protest in New York against Dean Rusk. Gold's increasing frustration with the inability of the movement to effect change convinced him of the need for ever more violent actions.

Terry Robbins was from Ohio and had been a prime mover in the SDS chapter at Kent State University. One of the most radical in Ohio, the chapter staged militant protests in this conservative town. Robbins had held national office in the SDS, but his frustration with the ever worsening political situation led him to join Weatherman. A fan of Bob Dylan's music, it was Gold who had suggested the name Weatherman for the organization.

After the townhouse explosion, the FBI broke down the doors of many of those who had been in Weather in its early days. A group of agents in New York, known as Squad 47, broke into the houses of relatives and friends of Weather members in search of information about the fugitives. Multiple warrants were issued for interstate flight and possession of explosives and by year's end six Weather people were on the FBI's Ten-Most-Wanted list, which the Justice Department then increased to sixteen to accommodate the new breed of political criminal.

Indictments came down on March 17, 1970, charging twelve Weather people with actions related to the Days of Rage. The most serious of these charges was conspiracy to cross state lines with the intent to incite a riot – the same charge that was made against the Chicago 8. Furthermore, the same federal judge – Julius Hoffman – was chosen to preside over the trial. The twelve indicted included most of Weather's leaders: Bernardine Dohrn, Mark Rudd, Jeff Jones, Mark Spiegel, Linda Evans, Judy Clark, Kathy Boudin, Bill Ayers, John Jacobs, Howie Machtinger, Lawrence Weiss, and Terry Robbins. Weather had no intention of appearing on the charges.[7]

In early April, after Larry Grathwohl tipped off the FBI, Dianne Donghi and Linda Evans were arrested for attempting to forge checks using their false identifications. Both women were released later that day, but their brush with the law convinced other Weather people involved in similar activities to obtain money (like selling drugs) to stop.

● ● ●

The movement in support of the New Haven Panther defendants – Bobby Seale and Ericka Huggins – was one of the more important battles of 1970. It was the first truly popular effort in the United States since the campaign to free Black Panther leader Huey Newton, which had linked the repression of the black liberation movement and the rise of fascism in America with the worldwide anti-imperialist struggle. Weatherman had long ago insisted on their inseparability and now, because of the egregiousness of the state's actions, thousands took up the struggle. A week of actions was planned at Yale University in New Haven, leading up to May Day. The mainstream media sensationalized the trial and the plans of protest organizers, as groups all along the East Coast worked together to bring about a large, militant action in solidarity with the defendants, the Panthers, and political prisoners in general. The state put thousands of troops on alert and assembled hundreds of police from all available agencies. The administration at Yale, meanwhile, worked frantically to head off any violence, with the president of the university, Kingman Brewster, even going so far as to uncharacteristically question the possibility of any Panther getting a fair trial in the United States.

To Weather, there was no doubt about the impossibility of

The New York Panther 21 support rally, spring 1970. Photograph from the Roz Payne Archives, reproduced courtesy of Roz Payne.

a fair trial. Yet the group remained publicly silent until three weeks after the Yale demonstrations. When Weather finally spoke, its statement expressed solidarity with "Eldridge, H. Rap Brown, and all black revolutionaries who first inspired us by their fight."[8] Interestingly, yet not surprising, was the mention of Cleaver and Brown, but not the Oakland-based Panthers. It seems fair to say that this was not only because of Cleaver's support of Weatherman after the Days of Rage, but also the result of Weather's decision not to organize in the streets, but to cause chaos from underground. Both Cleaver and Brown (who was not a Panther) favored such an approach, believing, like Weather, that the time was right for armed revolution and, moreover, that arms *were* the revolution.

The night of April 30th is Walpurgis Night. For practitioners of the Black Arts this is the unholiest night of the year – the best night to cast spells and conjure demonic powers.

On the night of April 30, 1970 President Nixon announced that American and South Vietnamese forces were advancing into Cambodia. Their purpose was to locate and destroy the headquarters of N. Vietnamese and NLF forces alleged to be hidden in Eastern Cambodia. This move, despite the administration's denials, is clearly an interference into the civil war raging between the Lon Nol government and its enemies. As in Vietnam, the United States has sent its troops into a civil war in order to shore up the crumbling position of a puppet regime.

Walt Crowley[9]

Within hours of the announcement of the US invasion of Cambodia, streets and campuses across the US and in several

European cities were filled with demonstrators. Thousands protested – holding rallies, trashing ROTC buildings, recruiting offices, and stores, closing down streets, and fighting with police. At Yale, the ad hoc steering committee of the Free Bobby and Ericka actions (the Panthers Bobby Seale and Ericka Huggins) held an emergency meeting and approved a call for a nationwide student strike. At the University of Maryland, the ROTC building was burned to the ground. At the University of Washington, demonstrations of a few hundred quickly developed into a takeover by thousands of people of the interstate highway near the campus, and, at Kent State in Ohio, after three days of rallies and insurrection (including the destruction of the ROTC building), national-guard troops opened fire on protestors, killing four. Those deaths caused the movement against the invasion to expand exponentially. Eventually, close to half of the colleges in the United States and many high-school campuses closed. In the military, GIs and dependents throughout the world expressed their solidarity with the protestors by refusing to fight and wearing black armbands.[10] Within the next two weeks police forces killed six blacks in Augusta, Georgia during civil-rights disturbances there, and, on May 14, they killed two black youths – a student and a delivery boy who was watching the protests – at Jackson State College in Mississippi during anti-war actions there. The state of crisis in the country was such that Nixon curtailed his war plans and, under heavy pressure from his more pragmatic advisors and anti-war liberals in the Congress, promised to withdraw US troops from Cambodia within sixty days.

The mainstream anti-war movement responded by calling for a massive demonstration in Washington, D.C. On May 9 a few hundred thousand protestors showed up at the Capitol for a rally. The rally's sponsors discouraged militance because they hoped that a peaceful demonstration would convince middle America and the Congress that it was time to end the war. The most militant action of the day was the takeover of the Peace Corps offices. According to one participant, although there were "10,000 people ready to occupy government buildings that day," no similar actions occurred.[11]

Weather was impressed by the general militance and anti-imperialist nature of most of the spring actions and, in a communiqué distributed on May 21, it expressed solidarity with the dead in Kent, Jackson, and Augusta and applauded the actions of white youth at the TDA demonstrations in February and during the nationwide response to the invasion of Cambodia. The letter, which was signed "Weatherman Underground," began: "Hello. This is Bernardine Dohrn, I'm going to read a declaration of a state of war." For the first time Weather embraced the revolutionary elements of the counterculture: "Freaks are revolutionaries," it wrote, "and revolutionaries are freaks." Because of the growing "alienation and contempt that young people [had] for this country", it finally believed such a step was possible. Asserting that the widespread use of illegal drugs made thousands of youth outlaws, the communiqué called on those youth to join the struggle. Dohrn wrote that there were hundreds of Weather people underground and in the names of Diana Oughton, Ted Gold, and Terry Robbins she promised that Weather would "never go back."[12]

The idea of the youth culture as an outlaw culture was romantic and alluring, but made for difficulties, as the state, perceiving the revolutionary aims of the counter-culture, was determined to silence it. With Vice-President Agnew as its mouthpiece, the Nixon administration attacked rock music, while the Justice Department and the Internal Revenue Service pressured Columbia Records and RCA to stop advertising in the underground press, which had the effect of putting many papers out of business. FBI memos stated that "Columbia Records's financial assistance . . . appears to be giving active aid and comfort to enemies of the United States."[13] The FBI and other law-enforcement agencies raided underground press offices around the country, destroying their equipment and confiscating their subscription lists. In addition, government harassment of counter-culture personalities intensified; for example, John Lennon's increasing outspokenness on political issues was met with deportation proceedings and John Sinclair, of the counter-cultural revolutionary group, the White Panthers, was sentenced to ten years in jail for giving two marijuana cigarettes as a gift to an undercover narcotics agent.

The seriousness with which the government took the youthful New Left, especially Weather, was apparent in the arrest on April 15 of the Weather woman Linda Evans on a Days of Rage indictment. Larry Grathwohl, who arranged the bust, described the intense pressure he was under from FBI headquarters to obtain an arrest, so intense, in fact, that the agency blew Grathwohl's cover in order to do so.[14]

Grathwohl had been under suspicion in Weatherman for weeks due to a couple of poorly explained absences. In addition, his questions about details of the cell's future plans were making his companions increasingly nervous. The bust came on the morning of April 15, when Grathwohl met Linda Evans at a diner in New York City. After she finished her breakfast, they left the diner and were immediately approached by an FBI agent who put them both under arrest. The two ran down the block but were quickly tackled and handcuffed by at least a dozen other agents who had been waiting in various parked vehicles. They were then placed in two different cars and taken to the FBI offices in Manhattan. After a short time there, during which Dianne Donghi was arrested by two other agents at the hotel room where she had spent the night before with Grathwohl, he and Evans were taken to the Federal Building in downtown Manhattan, once again riding in different cars. They were immediately arraigned, Grathwohl using his false identity of Thomas Neiman. Then they were brought to the holding cells in the building's basement. Donghi was already there and Evans was placed in the same cell with her. Grathwohl, handcuffed, remained standing outside the cells in full view of the two women. A marshal, unaware of Grathwohl's status as an informer, searched him again and found a dogtag Grathwohl had taped to the inside of his shoe after the townhouse explosion to insure that he would be properly identified if he was killed. The marshal read the dogtag and immediately accused Grathwohl of lying about his real name. The other marshal present, a supervisor, who knew that Grathwohl was working for the FBI, quickly grabbed the dogtag from his subordinate and insisted that Grathwohl's name really was Neiman. The fact that the supervisor did not question the discrepancy between Grathwohl's dogtag and the name he gave the judge was enough to confirm Evans's and Donghi's suspicions – Grathwohl was working for the FBI. Evans and Donghi were later released.

● ● ●

In its May 21 declaration of war, Weather promised to attack "a symbol of Amerikan injustice"[15] within fourteen days. When the time came and went with no attack, some in the

New Left were disappointed. After all, explained a letter addressed to Weatherman in the *Berkeley Tribe*, "Raising people's hopes that high isn't a good way to build trust in the underground."[16] However, at 7.00 p.m. on June 9, a series of explosions ripped through the second floor of the New York City police headquarters. According to police reports, the blast had the force of 10–15 sticks of dynamite and may have been caused by TNT. Seven people were injured and damage was estimated in the hundreds of thousands of dollars. The police had to move some of their men and operations elsewhere. The brief statement sent to the press expressed solidarity with radical youth of all backgrounds and challenged the authorities: "The pigs try to look invulnerable, but we keep finding their weaknesses ... They look for us – we get to them first."[17] A little over a month later, on July 26, to commemorate the anniversary of the Cuban revolution, Weatherman set off a small bomb at a military-police guard post at the Presidio Army base in San Francisco. This attack was coordinated with smaller actions around the country which were most likely conducted by a combination of Weather members and their allies in the revolutionary movement. One of these actions, which was announced in advance by a person claiming to be a Weather member, was a small explosion at a Bank of America branch in Manhattan. In both the San Francisco and New York bombings, damage was slight and involved nothing more than some shattered windows. In its July 26 communiqué sent from Detroit, Weather wrote: "Today we attack with riots, rocks and bombs the greatest killer-pig known to man – Amerikan imperialism."[18]

More federal indictments were handed down on July 23, charging thirteen Weather members with "conspiracy to bomb police stations and government buildings across the

A communiqué from Weatherman claiming responsibility for the bombing of the New York City Police headquarters in June 1970. From the collection of Will Miller, reproduced courtesy of *Liberated Guardian*.

A 1970 FBI "WANTED" poster showing many of the famous
Weatherman activists. Photograph from the Roz Payne Archives,
reproduced courtesy of Roz Payne.

Naomi Esther Jaffe
W/F, 27, 5-2, 105
dk brn hair, brn eyes

Jeffrey Carl Jones
W/M, 23, 5-11, 150
blond hair, blue eyes

David Benjamin Klafter
W/M, 23, 5-9, 150
brn hair, brn eyes

Howard N. Machtinger
W/M, 23, 5-10, 150
brn hair, green eyes

Celeste M. McCullough
W/F, 23, 5-4/5-5, 120
brn hair, brn eyes

Wendy Jane Panken
W/F, 21, 5-5, 125
brn hair, brn eyes

Robert Henry Roth
W/M, 20, 5-8, 130
brn hair, brn eyes

Mark William Rudd
W/M, 23, 5-11, 170
brn hair, blue eyes

Michael Louis Spiegel
W/M, 24, 6-1, 185
brn hair, brn eyes

Caroline M. Tanner
W/F, 21, 5-2, 135
brn hair, blue eyes

Lawrence Michael Weiss
W/M, 22, 6-1, 175
brn hair, hazel eyes

Cathlys P. Wilkerson
W/F, 25, 5-6, 110-115
brn hair, brn eyes

US." Dianne Donghi, Linda Evans, and Russell Neufeld – three of the persons named in the indictments – were arrested soon after. Donghi was arrested at the poverty center she worked at in New York and Neufeld was picked up at a hospital where he worked in Chicago. All three had been with Grathwohl during his stay in Detroit shortly after the war council in December 1969. In an attempt to legitimize Grathwohl in Weather's eyes, he was also named in these indictments. The remaining nine indictees were Mark Rudd, Bernardine Dohrn, Bill Ayers, Kathy Boudin, Cathy Wilkerson, Jane Spiegelman, Naomi Jaffe, Ronald Fliegelman, and Robert (Bo) Burlingham. All but Jaffe, Spiegelman, and Burlingham were already wanted for charges on the March 1970 indictments. Evans and Donghi opted to work for Weather aboveground after their court appearances. Several years later the indictments were discarded because of the illegality of FBI and police procedures.

Under the direction of the Internal Security Division of the Justice Department, local police continued their campaign of harassment and illegal procedures. Beginning in the spring of 1970, lawyer Mark Lefcourt – who was working on several cases involving former Weather members – had his office broken into several times and his home twice by police acting illegally. Another example of illegal police activity is the case of Robert Swartout, named as a coconspirator in the Days of Rage but not indicted. Early in 1970 he was kidnapped by Chicago police, beaten and tortured, and then sent on a plane to Virginia. When Swartout disembarked, he expected to be arrested, but nothing ever happened. The testimony the police had extracted from him under torture, however, was presented as evidence in the indictments against Weather members issued in July.[19]

Dianne Marie Donghi (right) and Jane Spiegelman at the New York Federal Court, July 28, 1970. Both were charged with conspiring to commit bombings. Photograph reproduced courtesy of UPI/Corbis-Bettmann.

Around this time, the White House and the Justice Department tried to combine various agencies – the FBI, the CIA, the Internal Revenue Service, the National Security Agency, the Defense Intelligence Agency, and Military Intelligence – with state and local red (political surveillance) squads in a program named after its designer John Huston to crush domestic opposition to US policies. Because of differences of opinion within the domestic police/intelligence apparatus, however, especially from FBI Director J. Edgar Hoover, who feared a loss of power, the plan was suspended, although many of its elements were put into practice in a newly formed unit directed by White House counsel John Dean – the Intelligence Evaluation Committee.[20] In fact, the failure of the Huston plan:

> had little effect upon the intelligence services: the CIA mail-opening went on; NSA selection of international communications expanded; the FBI opened thousands of new cases on domestic dissenters and intensified its campus surveillance . . .; the intelligence agencies formed a permanent intelligence committee . . .; and the intelligence directors continued to seek the full implementation of certain Huston plan provisions.[21]

By the summer of 1970 more than two thousand federal agents were involved in the campaign to destroy the New Left, the Panthers, the American Indian Movement, and other third-world groups.

Paradoxically, while Weather's aboveground supporters were subject to continual harassment and threats, the fugitives themselves moved about with minimal interference from the law. As they related in a letter in *The Last Supplement to the*

Whole Earth Catalog: "we do move around freely."[22] Even if there was a brush with police, because of a traffic stop, say, their false identifications were effective enough, so that no suspicions were aroused. Ayers later remarked, however, that every day he woke up thinking: "I wonder how many times I'll be nervous today."[23]

• • •

On February 19, 1970, Timothy Leary, the Harvard psychologist turned high priest of the counter-culture, had been convicted in California for possession of two marijuana cigarette butts. This followed another conviction for possession of less than a half-ounce of marijuana in Texas. In California, he was denied appeal and sentenced to ten years in prison. After further attempts by his lawyers to gain an appeal, he eventually ended up at the California Men's Colony at San Luis Obispo. Almost immediately, he began plotting an escape, and Weatherman, through the persuasive efforts of one of its LSD suppliers (who knew Leary), decided to help him. The dealer was part of a mythic and shadowy organization of hashish and LSD smugglers, manufacturers, and dealers from California and Nepal known in the counter-culture as the Brotherhood of Eternal Love. The plan to help Leary would not only test Weather's underground network, it also proved the sincerity of its expressed desire to link up with the counter-culture.

On September 13, 1970, under cover of darkness, Leary moved hand over hand along a cable suspended over the fence round the prison until he reached a pole on the other side and slid down to freedom. He made his way to the highway and waited in a roadside ditch until a car stopped at a prearranged spot on the shoulder and a girl with long dark hair jumped out. Leary jumped in and the girl followed. He was on his way to freedom, thanks to the Weather people. As the car drove north, his fellow passengers helped him change clothes and dye his hair. He was also given a set of false identification papers. The clothes were left at a rest stop where another car picked them up and then left them at another rest stop about 100 miles south of San Luis Obispo. This was done to persuade the police that Leary had headed for Mexico instead of the north. Leary switched vehicles once more that night before arriving at a safe house in North Oakland.[24]

Later that morning, as he rode north from Oakland, a car full of long-haired young people passed, honking and waving. Leary was naturally nervous at being recognized, but relaxed when he was told it was Mark Rudd and some friends in the other car.[25] Leary's destination was a camp on some Native American land in the northern Californian mountains. After arriving at a campsite near the native-owned land, Dohrn and two Weather men talked with representatives of the Native American nation about letting Leary spend the night there. Leary waited with two Weather women smoking marijuana and listening to a recording of the Grateful Dead. He was allowed to remain on the land for the night and part of the following day. He then rode with another Weather member, identified only as Frank, to a motel. Finally, almost four days after his escape, he was moved to a ranch house somewhere in northern California where he and his wife Rosemary were temporarily reunited. Less than three days later, after receiving another set of false papers to replace the first, he was in Algeria. His wife met him again soon afterwards, having taken a different route.

Weatherman, in a perfectly executed plan, had freed

Timothy Leary from prison. Its ability to get Leary out of the country and into the Panther compound in Algeria was proof of its effective underground network. Although it is unclear exactly how many Weather members there were (estimates ranged from 100 to Dohrn's claim of several hundred), its network included many New Left and counter-culture radicals, both from other organizations and unaffiliated individuals. Although some support groups, such as the Mad Dogs from New York, were relatively organized, most supporters were individuals who approved of some aspect of Weather's program and helped in what ever way they could, whether that meant carrying a banner expressing solidarity with Weather at a demonstration, publishing a Weather statement in a newspaper, or providing temporary refuge for a Weather figure.

For example, activists Stew and Judith (Gumbo) Albert of Berkeley were instrumental in arranging Leary's stay in the Panther compound in Algeria. The distribution of Weather's next communiqué, like the one written to celebrate the Cuban revolution on July 26, was facilitated with help from the White Panthers, and Yippies. As Leary wrote in his description of the escape: "They [Weather] are not in hiding, but are invisible." Weather was "in every tribe, commune, dormitory, farmhouse, barracks and townhouse where kids are making love, smoking dope, preparing for the future."[26]

The beginnings of an alliance of "Leary's upper middle class white following . . . with the militant whites, the blacks, and the Hispanic lower and middle class" was in the offing. Both Weatherman and the Cleaver wing of the Panthers had been working hard to effect just such a coalition, especially after the two organizations realized they shared similar analyses of the revolutionary situation in the United States.[27]

The Leary escape marked the beginning of a new strategy for Weather. The deaths in the March 6 townhouse explosion forever "destroyed their belief that armed struggle is the only real revolutionary struggle."[28] In its place was a new strategy which, as Dohrn told Leary before he left for Algeria, did not exclude armed struggle but accepted its use only "when it was forced upon us."[29] Leary, meanwhile, released a public letter in which he called on the counter-culture to resist and, using the horrors inflicted by the Nazis as an example, urged its adherents not to allow themselves to be led "peacefully to the slaughter like those at Auschwitz." He supported Weather's declaration of war and warned, "Do not be deceived. It is a classic stratagem of genocide to camouflage their [the government's] wars as law and order police actions."[30]

● ● ●

On August 7, 1970, Jonathan Jackson, the 17-year-old brother of prison revolutionary George Jackson, entered the Marin County courthouse armed with a submachine gun. He hoped to force the release of the Soledad Brothers – George Jackson, Fleeta Drumgo, and John Clutchette, who were charged with the murder of two guards at Soledad Prison after guards had killed another prisoner. Jonathan gave guns to three prisoners who were present in court – Ruchell Magee, a jailhouse lawyer who was testifying at the trial of fellow prisoner James McClain, and William Christmas. The three then took the judge, the prosecutor, and three jurors hostage. They left the courthouse and placed the hostages in a county van. Before the armed men and their hostages left the courthouse, the Marin County sheriff had ordered his men not to shoot, but the van was hit by a hail of gunfire from San Quentin prison guards and other law-enforcement personnel immediately after it left the building's garage. Jackson, Judge Haley, McClain, and Christmas were all killed. Several weeks later, at approximately 1:30 in the morning on October 8, Weather exploded a bomb at the courthouse building in anger over the "murders." The explosion wrecked one of the courtrooms in the building and an adjacent bathroom.

In a rare display of humor, on October 5, Weather blew up the police statue in Haymarket Square for the second time. The accompanying communiqué – released on October 10 – called for a fall offensive of youth resistance to "blast away the myth of superiority of the man."[31] On October 9, at approximately 1:30 in the morning, Weather exploded a bomb at the Long Island court building in solidarity with a prison uprising in New York City jails which had just ended in a violent put-down. The prisoners, including some of the New York Panther 21, had taken control of the jails for up to five days. They also held thirty-two hostages, who were released unharmed after New York mayor John Lindsay promised no reprisals. Weather's bomb attack was preceded in this instance by a phone call, and the bomb itself was placed in a phone booth near the building, which was damaged so extensively that it was put out of action. According to the police the bomb was comparable to that at the police headquarters building in June that year. Weather's communiqué on October 9 expressed solidarity with the growing revolutionary movements in the prisons and, at the same time, advised America's youth not to fall for the lies put out by the system. It emphasized the need to build the youth culture into a culture of insurgency that would resist the genocide of the Vietnamese and of America's blacks.

In another action related to the fall offensive, on October

14, the Proud Eagle Tribe (later renamed the Women's Brigade of Weather) exploded a bomb at the Center for International Affairs at Harvard University. This, the first attack by an all-women's grouping in Weather, was in reaction to, and solidarity with, the arrest of activist Angela Davis earlier in the day on charges of interstate flight and conspiracy to commit murder. These charges, which were related to her support of George Jackson, were based on the fact that one of the guns used by Jackson's brother Jonathan in the abortive attempt to free the Soledad Brothers was registered in her name. (Davis was eventually acquitted on both charges.) "The fall offensive has begun," read the women's statement. "We *all* want to build a militant women's movement that commits itself to the destruction of US imperialism."[32]

This communication dated December 6, 1970, arrived special delivery in the Liberation News Service office in New York on December 10. The two stamps on the envelope commemorated Tom Paine and Lucy Stone. The first page of the document has a hand-painted rainbow with a red lightning arrow. A Vietnamese stamp is in the right hand corner. The stamp shows a Vietnamese woman dressed in green, with a rifle over her shoulder. "New Morning, Changing Weather" is painted in black ink above the rainbow.

The document is signed Weather Underground, and Bernardine Dohrn.

Editor's note attached to the "New Morning" communiqué[33]

On December 10, a Weather communiqué entitled "New Morning, Changing Weather" reached the LNS office in New York and was released to underground papers across the nation. This was the first statement from the organization that did not accompany any specific action. To verify its authenticity, Bernardine Dohrn had signed it in longhand. The statement was a review of Weather's past errors and its hopes for the future. For the first time, Weather publicly acknowledged its earlier opinions as alienating to those outside the organization. It called its "tendency to consider only bombings or picking up the gun as revolutionary, with the glorification of the heavier the better" a military error. With a new maturity in both approach and analysis, the letter provided the rest of the revolutionary New Left with a glimpse of the struggles in the collectives since Weatherman's conception. Foremost among them were the questions of the youth culture's place in the revolution and the role of women in the organization.

As in much of the New Left, Weather continued to argue over the youth culture's revolutionary nature. Some members still insisted that the culture was merely an exercise in bourgeois decadence, but others believed it to be the beginnings of a "young, and unformed society (nation)." By the time "New Morning" was published, the latter argument had become the Weather line, as evidenced by their role in the Leary escape. Furthermore, the statement revealed Weather's growing belief in structures of leadership and organization which emphasized the holistic nature of their lives as revolutionaries. "The revolution involves our whole lives," the communiqué stated. "We are not part-time soldiers or secret revolutionaries."

This new organizational approach precipitated a stronger role for women and, as the October 14 action at Harvard made clear, the formation of some all-women units. Men, who had previously held a good deal of power in the organization, now found themselves on a more equal footing with

Communique Nº 2

TONIGHT, AT 7 P.M., WE BLEW UP THE N.Y.C. POLICE HEADQUARTERS. WE CALLED IN A WARNING BEFORE THE EXPLOSION.

THE PIGS IN THIS COUNTRY ARE OUR ENEMIES. THEY HAVE MURDERED FRED HAMPTON AND TORTURED JOAN BIRD. THEY ARE RESPONSIBLE FOR 6 BLACK DEATHS IN AUGUSTA, 4 MURDERS IN KENT STATE, THE IMPRISONMENT OF LOS SIETE DE LA RAZA IN SAN FRANCISCO AND THE CONTINUAL BRUTALITY AGAINST LATIN AND WHITE YOUTH ON THE LOWER EAST SIDE. SOME ARE NAMED MITCHELL AND AGNEW. OTHERS CALL THEMSELVES LEARY AND HOGAN. THE NAMES ARE DIFFERENT BUT THE [CRIMES]

A Weather Report sent AP Friday, June 10 (PM)

women. As if to underline the new gender roles, the statement was signed Weather Underground, not Weatherman or Weatherman Underground, as in the past. In contrast to the heavy-handed tactics employed by the earlier male leadership, it stated, the strategies developed through the women's initiatives emphasized struggle and flexibility. Noting that people "became revolutionaries in the schools, in the army, in the prisons, in communes, and on the streets [and] not in an underground cell," the letter defined Weather as part of a "nation," not a separate organization.[34] Bernardine's sister, Jennifer – who worked aboveground with allies of Weather – later made the observation that the "New Morning" statement "demystified [Weather] a lot . . . and it was the beginning of a sense that they're really another whole arm, a whole base for our movement."[35] The result was that Weather would no longer organize as collectives, but as "families" instead. Families were defined as composed of people who had developed bonds beyond politics. After all, went part of the reasoning, "it's harder [for informants] to live in a family without being detected."[36] It was a step which had been promoted by many in Weather since 1968, when the Ann Arbor faction of SDS spoke of a sense of community coming from revolutionary struggles.

"New Morning" acknowledged the military ineffectiveness of Weather's bombings until then by comparing them to a bee sting, and yet it emphasized their political and social effect: "The world knows that even the white youth of Babylon will resort to force to bring down imperialism."[37] And indeed the state acknowledged the problems posed by Weather in its continuing campaign to capture its members. Only one week after the release of "New Morning," Judy Clark was arrested in a New York movie theater on charges listed in the Days of

Rage indictments. Her bail was set at $75,000. She was then taken to Chicago, where Judge Hoffman added another $150,000 to the sum.

NOTES

1. Robin Morgan, "Goodbye To All That", *Rat*, February 6, 1970.
2. Ibid.
3. Bread and Roses Collective, quoted in H. Jacobs, ed., *Weatherman*, Ramparts Press, Berkeley, Cal., 1970, p. 327.
4. "Letter from a Weathersister," *Rat*, February 6, 1970.
5. Kirkpatrick Sale, *SDS*, Vintage, New York, 1973, p. 647.
6. Weather Underground, "New Morning, Changing Weather," Weatherman communiqué, December 6, 1970.
7. The indictments, which came from Detroit, were the result of undercover investigations and just plain fabrication.
8. *Liberated Guardian*, May 1970.
9. Walt Crowley, "On Strike," *The Helix*, Seattle, May 1970.
10. This is from the author's recollections of his youth spent on military bases with his father, a soldier. From March 1970 until June 1973 he lived in Frankfurt, West Germany, and attended high school there.
11. *Quicksilver Times*, May 19, 1970.
12. *Liberated Guardian*, May 1970. Weather furthered the concept of the political outlaw in its "Letter to Brother Dan" (Berrigan), October 8, 1970. This letter was written as Weather members watched Berrigan's arrest on television on charges of destruction of draft files.
13. Abe Peck, *Uncovering the Sixties: The Life and Times of the Underground Press*, Pantheon, New York, 1985, p. 176.
14. Larry Grathwohl, *Bringing down America: An FBI Informer with the Weathermen*, Arlington House, New Rochelle, N.Y., 1976, p. 179.
15. *Liberated Guardian*, May 1970.
16. *Berkeley Tribe*, June 12, 1970.
17. Weatherman Underground, "Communiqué Number 2," June 9, 1970.
18. Weatherman "Communiqué Number 4."
19. Frank Donner, *The Age of Surveillance*, Alfred Knopf, New York, 1980, pp. 371–2.
20. The Justice Department was also involved in running this unit, which was disbanded after the Watergate revelations began to strangle the White House counter-intelligence operations.
21. Select Committee to Study Government Operation with Respect to Intelligence Activities, *Supplementary Detailed Staff Reports on Intelligence Activities and the Rights of Americans, Book III Final Report*, United States Government Printing Office, Washington, D.C., 1976, p. 980.
22. Weather Underground, "From the Weather Bureau," *The Last Supplement*

to the *Whole Earth Catalog*, ed. Ken Kesey and Paul Krassner, Whole Earth Catalog, Menlo Park, Cal., 1971, p. 20.

23. *Underground*, directed by Emile DeAntonio, with Mary Wexler and members of Weather Underground Organization, First Run Features, New York, 1976.

24. Timothy Leary, *Confessions of a Hope Fiend*, Bantam, New York, 1973, p. 124.

25. Staff, "Rap with J. Dohrn," *The Seed*, 1971.

26. Leary, *Confessions*, p. 137.

27. Leary was eventually expelled from the Panther compound in Algeria, primarily because of his refusal to go along with Panther demands that he conduct himself in such a way as not to attract any more law enforcement attention than the compound already received. After his expulsion, he and his female partner at the time (an informer) traveled around the globe and were eventually arrested by drug-enforcement agents in Afghanistan. Rumors abounded that Leary traded information on Weather safe houses for a shorter prison term. The rumors were never substantiated, but did diminish Leary's credibility in the counter-culture. He ended up serving just over two years in Folsom Prison, California.

28. "New Morning, Changing Weather," Weatherman communiqué, December 6, 1970.

29. Leary, *Confessions*, p. 138.

30. Quoted from a letter from Leary in appendices in Jacobs, ed., *Weatherman*, p. 517.

31. Weather communiqué, October 10, 1970.

32. Women's Brigade statement, October 14, 1970.

33. Liberation News Service, December 10, 1970.

34. Weather Underground, "New Morning, Changing Weather," December 10, 1971.

35. Jennifer Dohrn, "A Rap With Jennifer Dohrn," *Chicago Seed*, April 1971.

36. "New Morning, Changing Weather."

37. Ibid.

6...

Changing
Weather

Was the "New Morning, Changing Weather" statement as dramatic a shift in Weather philosophy as it appeared? Or was it merely the same philosophy cloaked in the rhetoric of the counter-culture. After all, Weather had acknowledged the revolutionary potential of the youth culture in "You Don't Need a Weatherman." But the actions and writings of late 1970 demonstrate its first genuine acceptance of the counter-culture as a revolutionary entity in and of itself. In fact, the "New Morning" statement took its title from a just released album by Bob Dylan. Both the album and the statement shared a reflective, yet resolute mood.

In San Francisco, where the counter-culture and New Left politics first came together publicly at the Human Be-In in January 1967, Weather's recognition of the counter-culture brought a musical response. Two leaders of the rock band the Jefferson Airplane – Grace Slick and Paul Kantner – joined other rock musicians on the album *Sunfighter*, which was dedicated to the victims of the townhouse explosion and included a song for Diana Oughton eulogizing "Weatherwoman Diana."

Others in the revolutionary Left, most notably some members of the New York Panther 21, criticized the "New Morning" statement for what was perceived as a lack of militancy, and cautioned Weather not to confuse the revolutionary and hedonistic aspects of the counter-culture. Based on their own experience with drugs and drug-users, and specifically relating the proportionate increase in drug availability to the decrease in revolutionary activity in the community, these Panthers warned Weather that "grass and organic consciousness expanding drugs [were] not weapons of the revolution."[1] Although drugs had played a role in the development of a sense of community, wrote the Panthers, the fact that they were made so readily available to the youth community implied their counter-revolutionary potential. After all, it is much harder to think and organize if one is high on LSD or marijuana. Contrasting the building of community to the fighting of a revolution, the New York Panthers emphasized their belief that revolution was the only way to oppose the repression of the community. To settle for less insured the culture's impotence not only in changing the greater reality, but even in defending itself.

It was over the question of drugs and their role in developing revolutionary consciousness that the counter-culture and the New Left most disagreed. Although marijuana and LSD opened youth to new ways of perceiving the world, they also, so the Left argued, exacerbated the individualistic ethic of the dominant culture within the counter-culture. What Weather, the Yippies, and other political groups hoped to do – taking their lead from the Panthers and Young Lords – was to develop a new ethic within the counter-culture which would encourage drug-users and sellers to do what was best for the community: a sense of responsibility to one's peers, if you will. Ideally what this meant was that no "death drugs" (speed, cocaine, heroin, pcp) – or, as Weather labeled them in "New Morning," the enemy's allies – would be sold.

We have attacked the Capitol because it is, along with the White House and the Pentagon, the worldwide symbol of the government which is now attacking Indochina. To millions of people here and in Latin America, Africa, and Asia, it is a monument to US domination over the planet. The invaders of Laos will not have peace in this country.

Weather Underground, Communiqué 8, February 28, 1971

In the first major Weather action of 1971, a bomb was exploded in the US Capitol building in response to the invasion and public bombing of Laos (*public* because, as the Pentagon Papers show, Laos in fact had been under attack by the US military since before the Johnson administration). The action was carried out by two teams of volunteers and is one of the few Weather bombings ever specifically discussed by the organization in a public forum.

After the teams were chosen by group consensus – arrived at, one assumes, in telephone and personal conversations – they were given specific tasks: one team scouted the target area and provided detailed information to the other team, which placed the explosives. In fact two bombs were placed in the Capitol. The first one on February 28, was thought to have been placed on a ledge where in reality no such ledge existed and fell several feet, so that the explosive device did not ignite. The next evening, March 1, it was decided to risk bringing another device into the building. So the same Weather members went back into the Capitol building and set a smaller device on top of the previous one. This time the bomb exploded and ignited the larger device placed earlier. Earlier telephone calls to the media warning them about the action (hence the February 28 date on the communiqué)had apparently been ignored; now, another informed the Capitol police that: "You will get many calls like this, but this one is real. This building will blow in 30 minutes."[2]

The strident language of the accompanying communiqué was typical of Weather statements of the past, but the political analysis it provided was more substantive. The choice of target located blame for the genocide in Indochina not just in the White House and the Pentagon but also in Congress. Dealing a slap in the face to the liberal wing of the anti-war movement, the bombing and the statement blamed the entire system, not just Nixon and Kissinger and the generals, for "the genocide against all Indochinese people who dare to fight against Amerikan imperialism." Weather confronted the lie put forth by Nixon and many Congress members that the Vietnamization of the war meant peace, and rejected the doublespeak that called the expanding air war a phased withdrawal. Vietnamization was a policy designed to hand over the bulk of the fighting on the ground to the South Vietnamese military, while the United States provided logistical support and even greater air power. The strategy was intended to decrease the number of American battle deaths and thereby end opposition to the war.

The communiqué went on to warn that "as Custer learned at Little Big Horn, as the French found out at DienBienphu, and as Nixon is learning in the Laotian hills west of KheSanh, the arrogance of the white man can lead to his own destruction." In response to the media myth that the anti-war movement had cooled off, the statement spoke of a new spirit in the streets: "All over the country revolutionaries are getting ready for the spring." No longer were those marching merely against the war; their experiences over the past few years, especially in May 1970, had drawn them closer to an anti-imperialist position. "Nixon," wrote Weather, "will see what he took for acquiescence was really the calm before the storm."

To many, Weather's position no longer seemed extreme, and the bombing was applauded by much of the New Left which saw it as a prelude to the massive anti-imperialist direct actions planned for the weeks of April 24 – May 6. The government, too, understood the connection and, in the weeks immediately following the Capitol attack, called members of the Mayday Tribe, the People's Coalition for Peace and Justice, Yippies, and other anti-war organizations before a grand jury in an attempt to criminalize the movement.

Reflecting on the state of the white anti-imperialist movement, Weather sounded hopeful in the communiqué. It acknowledged the role played by youth in the revolution and encouraged "all forms of organizing and political warfare to destroy the Amerikan war machine." While other derivatives of the original RYM divided into smaller cells and argued about theoretical questions not considered relevant by the majority in the anti-imperialist movement, Weather finally became an accepted and even cherished part of it.

Weather's acceptance in the movement seems to have occurred because it no longer sought to assume the vanguard. The Panthers, too, underwent a change around this time which resulted in a split between the Oakland and New York branches of the party. According to most commentators, the split occurred primarily over differences regarding armed struggle and organizational approaches, as well as some personal conflicts. The Oakland faction (under Huey Newton's leadership) disagreed with the New York wing (under Cleaver's direction from Algeria) and continued to insist that armed warfare in the United States was suicide. From Newton's perspective, to engage in armed warfare would only isolate the party and insure its destruction by the state. The government, of course, relished the dissension in the party, which its agents encouraged, for example with death threats against Huey Newton purported to have been written by various New York Panthers but actually composed by the FBI.[3]

• • •

Two weeks prior to the bombing of the Capitol building, a group of anti-war youth organized by the National Student Association met in Ann Arbor, Michigan, to facilitate the adoption of a peace treaty formulated and signed by students and youth from the United States and Vietnam. The treaty was similar to the one then proposed by the NLF and virtually identical to the one eventually signed by both North Vietnam and the United States in January 1973 in Paris. Its implementation was demanded by the Mayday Tribe – one of the main organizers of the anti-war demonstrations planned for the late spring in Washington, D.C. It was a demand from the American and Vietnamese people to the US government to stop the war; and the chaos planned for the D.C. streets in May was the forum for the presentation of the treaty. The avowed purpose of the Washington Mayday demonstrations of 1971 was to stop the government from functioning. If the government ground to a halt, went the rationale, so would the war. With this ambitious intention in mind, the planners (among them Rennie Davis of the Chicago 8) called on counter-cultural revolutionaries to show up in Washington by May 1 and set up camp in West Potomac Park. Many of the participants came early for a series of other, mostly legal, anti-war actions called by an alphabet soup of organizaions under the leadership of the New Mobe. Separate from the demonstrations organized by the Mayday Tribe and the New Mobe were, notably, those sponsored by the Vietnam Veterans Against the War (VVAW), who arrived in D.C. in mid-April and ended their "temporary incursion into the state of Congress" with a mass return of their war medals.[4]

• • •

Mayday dawned with a crowd of more than 50,000 camped out in West Potomac Park. Since May 1 was a Saturday, the crowd spent the day planning actions for the following week, setting up communications – including a clandestine AM radio station – and dancing to the never ending music provided free by a multitude of local and national rock groups. On Sunday morning, after an all-night concert, police ordered those in the encampment to move. Some chose to stay and, after a couple of hours had passed, the police moved in and made the first of the week's 12,000 arrests.

By dawn on Monday, thousands of activists had begun to block streets leading to government offices, using their bodies, trash cans, junked cars, park benches, and whatever else they could find. The police, under direct orders from Attorney General John Mitchell, used clubs and tear gas liberally and arrested whomever they could catch. According to the *Quicksilver Times*, "Despite later public announcements in

A Mayday 1971 poster, from the cover of a spring 1971 edition of the
Eugene *Augur*. From the Labadie Collection, Special Collections
Library, University of Michigan, reproduced courtesy of the Library.

which police denied the success of Mayday, for almost five hours police and demonstrators played 'cat and mouse' with police often taking thirty or more minutes to arrive at and clear a newly snarled location." This, in itself, was not, as the police claimed, business as usual.[5]

Although the Mayday Tribe did not style itself as a revolutionary outfit, its writings and speeches were decidedly anti-imperialist and anti-racist. One small example can be found in the press release which consistently urged those coming to D.C. not to inconvenience the surrounding black community but to concentrate their efforts on disrupting the government. In addition, the Mayday Tribe linked the ongoing trials of black revolutionaries, specifically Bobby Seale and Ericka Huggins, to the fight against imperialism, even working with groups who were planning a rally in New Haven on May 7, 1971. (The rally was canceled, however, due to a change in defense strategy.)

During Mayday week, Weather issued an open letter to Mrs. Bacon, mother of the non-Weather woman Leslie Bacon charged with the Capitol bombing. It called the government's attempt to try Leslie who, according to Weather, was not involved in the bombing "a shallow attempt to spread fear among the thousands of free happy children in Washington angered and committed to end this racist war," and applauded the street actions. Weather acknowledged the differences in strategy in the movement and stated that in the differences lay strength "when we respect and affirm each other's passionate ways of acting to end the war,"[6] a thinly disguised reference to the attack on the Capitol which placed it in the context of the movement as a whole.

● ● ●

The insurgency in the prisons achieved its greatest triumphs and defeats in 1971. The growth of the movements in support of prison activists like the Soledad Brothers and of Angela Davis, and the dropping of all charges against Seale and Huggins in Connecticut, served as minor triumphs in the struggle against the American state. The murder of Black Panther and prison revolutionary George Jackson in August and the massacre at Attica State Penitentiary three weeks later were vicious reminders of just how far the state would go to preserve its power. The attack on the Marin County courthouse by Jonathan Jackson and others in August 1970 had brought the case of the Soledad Brothers international attention. Knowledge of the circumstances surrounding the incarceration of George Jackson and thousands of other black and Latino men and women in US jails leant weight to the perception that prisons were indeed "an appendage of the state apparatus employed to maintain exploitative and oppressive social conditions."[7] The indictments following the Marin County courthouse rescue attempt gained more attention for the prisoners especially because they included Angela Davis, who already had a worldwide following.

Since much of the support for the Soledad case was coordinated by the Panthers, the organizing was done in a revolutionary context. The fact of state violence in the prisons, and in the communities where the defendants came from, made it virtually impossible for liberal sympathizers and their press to redefine the struggle in non-revolutionary terms, since there was no denying the violence of the system in the daily lives of black people in the United States.

On August 21, 1971, George Jackson was shot to death in the yard at San Quentin prison in circumstances which remain a mystery to this day. As a tribute published by the

Berkeley Tribe stated: "We may never know exactly how he died. But we damn well know why he died." Expressing both disbelief at the act and its inevitability, the tribute placed the blame directly on the "criminally repressive and racist judicial system."[8]

One week later, on August 28, Weather attacked three offices of the California prison system in San Francisco, Sacramento, and San Mateo as a tribute to Jackson. The damage topped $100,000. In San Francisco, the blast destroyed the ground-floor offices of a psychiatric clinic for parolees and caused damage worth $50,000. The Sacramento explosion occurred in a seventeen-floor building and caused a comparable amount of damage. The interior of the building in San Mateo was rendered uninhabitable. Although published details about the implementation of the attacks do not exist, the Atlanta underground paper *Georgia Straight* reported that in the San Francisco bombing "someone went in after 5:00 closing and placed the bomb in an area which they had to crawl into."[9] The communiqué that followed addressed the history of black people in America, tracing the legacy of violence against them from the chains of the slave ships to the violence of the prisons, where a disproportionate number of black men and women found themselves once again in slavery, "paid pennies an hour to produce everything from shoes to missile parts." Weather compared US prisons to the strategic hamlets of Vietnam and drew an analogy between the removal of rebellious Vietnamese populations to the hamlets build under Operation Phoenix, and the removal of "the rebels of Watt, Harlem, Detroit" to strategic hamlets called prisons in the United States. Both relocations, it continued, were "an attempt to control colonial peoples."[10]

The murder of George Jackson was by no means the final

volley in the state's war against the revolutionary prison movement in 1971. In the early hours of September 13, a massacre by New York State police and other law-enforcement agencies took the lives of thirty-nine men at Attica State Penitentiary. The outcome of a five-day drama, the assault shocked even the most calloused revolutionaries.

The Attica Liberation Faction was formed in May 1971 in order to facilitate a more humane existence for the inmates of the prison. By July 2, a list of twenty-eight demands had been formulated and submitted to state officials, including Governor Nelson Rockefeller. The demands were not intrinsically revolutionary, but addressed issues dealing with the prisoners' daily lives. To those in control, however, any demand seemed threatening.

Nonetheless, liberals in the prison administration tried to implement what demands they could on their own, but their attempts were rejected or ignored by the warden and guards. Meanwhile, the prisoners continued to organize, forming study groups where the literate prisoners taught other prisoners to read and write. These study groups also provided opportunities for the inmates to discuss political ideas and the progress of their struggle for rights. The warden, after realizing the groups were empowering the prisoners, halted their activities.

The uprising began on September 9, after the beating of two prisoners the day before and the locking up of some others. Within minutes of the initial confrontation, forty guards were held hostage by the inmates, who also took control of a part of the prison known as D-Block. Although the original outbreak had much in common with other prison riots – with inmates beating guards and looting facilities – within an hour or so the uprising took on a revolutionary character.

The leadership quickly organized some men to guard the hostages from further harm and began listing prisoner demands. Five new demands were added to the original list the Attica Liberation Faction had presented to the governor in July. In their foreword to the list, the men addressed the people of America, saying, "The incident that erupted here at Attica is not the result of the dastardly bushwacking of two prisoners September 9, 1971, but of the unmitigated oppression wrought by the racist administrative network of the prison."[11] The five new demands included a call for amnesty; the reconstruction of the prison by inmates; immediate negotiation through a team chosen by the inmates and including movement lawyers, sympathetic members of the New York assembly, and journalists, representatives of the Panthers and Young Lords, and Louis Farrakhan of the Nation of Islam; federal intervention to implement the original demands; and transport for those men who wished to resettle in a non-imperialistic country.

An outside negotiating team was organized and, over the next three and a half days, worked with the prisoners and uncooperative state officials to ease the situation. Meanwhile, Governor Rockefeller ordered state police to prepare for a military assault on the prison. On September 13, after negotiations were abruptly ended and a call to surrender from the Commissioner of Corrections office was rejected by the men in D-Yard, "a choking cloud of CS gas fell abruptly over D-Yard . . . A shot rang out from a rooftop post . . . and a second . . . then a barrage . . ."[12] The toll was 39 dead: 30 inmates and 9 of the guards who had been held hostage. Less than half an hour later the uprising was over, and guards and troopers were forcing men to strip and lie face down on the ground while they brutally beat them.

Weather's response was quick and assured. Four days after the massacre, at a few minutes past 7:30 p.m., an explosion ripped through the cinderblock walls of a ninth-floor bathroom in a state-office building in Albany, N.Y. This floor housed the offices of the Commissioner of Corrections, Russell Oswald, the man who had given the order to the troopers on the 13th. Calls were made to the *Daily News*, the *Times-Union* of Albany, and the radio station WBAI minutes before the explosion. The newsroom staff of the Albany paper notified police at the building who finished clearing the premises seconds before the bomb went off.

In the accompanying statement, Weather placed the blame for the slaughter at Attica directly on the "society run by white racists," and traced the history of racist violence since the Second World War. It recalled the "four black girls killed by a bomb in Birmingham, the murder of students at Orangeburg, and Jackson," the numerous black uprisings and the murders of Malcolm X., Martin Luther King, Jr., Fred Hampton, and George Jackson, and repeatedly insisted that racism was the "main question white people have to face."[13]

● ● ●

On May 9, 1972, the United States sent two hundred planes over the northern half of Vietnam to mine its harbors and bomb the countryside. A day later the Hanoi delegation to the peace talks in Paris condemned the attack, saying the US had "taken the gravest step in the escalation of the war to date and thrown down an insolent challenge to the Vietnamese people."[14] Later the same day, the Senate passed a resolution against the escalation. By the afternoon of May 10, the police and anti-war protestors were confronting one another across the country. Streets were blocked in Chicago, College Park (Maryland), Binghamton (New York), and New Haven, to name just a few places. A contingent of Vietnam Veterans Against the War attempted to storm the United Nations in New York, and at the Capitol building more than thirty demonstrators were literally thrown out of the House galley for disrupting the proceedings.

The bombing of North Vietnam continued unabated for the next week and so did the protests. On May 11 alone, several hundred activists were arrested in various actions throughout the country. The National Peace Action Coalition and the People's Coalition for Peace and Justice, two pacifist groups, called for major demonstrations in D.C. the next weekend. In Madison, Wisconsin, a policeman was shot as he tried to arrest three protestors during anti-imperialist actions. At the University of New Mexico in Albuquerque, students were hit with birdshot when police opened fire on a crowd protesting the war. From Princeton, New Jersey, to Berkeley, California, and many points in between, the numbers of enraged activists continued to grow. A theatrical protest occurred in the Atlantic Ocean near Nixon's home in Key Biscayne, Florida: a flotilla of demonstrators dropped balloons in the water in a symbolic protest against the mining of Vietnamese harbors. Two were arrested when they ran through the military lines around the Nixon compound.

Like the Mayday actions of 1971, the demonstrations targeted corporations which made money from the war, proving the continuing influence of anti-imperialist thought in the movement. The mainstream anti-war movement, meanwhile, was in the control of left-wing democrats who were working hard for Senator McGovern. This latest effort to legitimize the anti-war movement also tended to further isolate its revolutionary elements, with the McGovern campaign diverting a great deal of the energy of the Left into electoral politics, much as the McCarthy campaign had in 1968.

Weather lent a revolutionary credence of its own to the protest when, on May 19, 1972 (Ho Chi Minh's birthday), the group exploded a bomb in the Air Force wing of the Pentagon. The bomb was placed in a women's restroom on the fourth floor. The blast devastated the restroom, blowing away a 30-foot section of the wall, breaking windows, and mangling the plumbing. The consequent flooding shut down a computer on the first floor which served as part of a military communications network spanning the globe. In addition, a computer tape archive containing highly classified information was severely damaged.[15] The inner sanctum of the war machine had been attacked.

Weather's action lifted many a revolutionary heart throughout the US and the rest of the world. In anti-war demonstrations in Frankfurt am Main, German youth cheered the action, chanting "Fur den sieg des Vietcong, Bomben auf das Pentagon" (For the victory of the VC, bomb the Pentagon) as they marched through the streets toward US military installations.[16] In the United States, many anti-imperialists privately applauded as they organized against the continued destruction of Vietnam by B-52 bombers. On the Monday following the explosion, under the watchful eyes of military and federal police, a non-violent people's blockade of the Pentagon was attempted. Due to poor planning by the organizers and an extra-large contingent of federal riot police on duty in the wake of the bombing, the blockade failed. Several hundred blockaders later attempted to maneuver through police lines, but the day ended with only twenty-five arrests.

The communiqué which accompanied the bombing lauded the ongoing offensive of the Vietnamese, stating the obvious: "the Thieu regime and the ARVN would collapse within a matter of days without US air and naval power."[17] Quoting bits of Ho Chi Minh's poetry, Weather provided its audience with a brief revolutionary history of Vietnam and praised the Vietnamese people's heroism and perseverance in the face of its various colonialist enemies over the years. Weather called the Vietnamization policy of the US government racist and decried the strategy which turned Asian against Asian. By emphasizing the racism implicit in US foreign policy, the communiqué hoped to slow the tacit acceptance of that policy in Vietnam, especially by youth previously against the war. Unfortunately, the cynical double-edged policy of Vietnamization and cooptation made the anti-imperialists' struggle to maintain a revolutionary movement much more difficult. Still, the inspiration of the Vietnamese lifted Weather's hopes in their fight against the US war.

Later in the year Weather attempted to organize another campaign supporting the NLF's final offensive, but failed to gain the support needed to carry it through. In the wake of that offensive, the United States carpetbombed North Vietnam throughout much of December – the infamous Christmas bombings. Nevertheless, on January 27, 1973, US and North Vietnamese negotiators signed a peace agreement which recognized the sovereignty, unity, and territorial integrity of Vietnam and called for a cessation of US involvement in South Vietnam. After pointing out the difference between a final victory in Vietnam and the victory represented by the signing of the peace treaty, Weather hailed the accords, urging "all opponents of the government's war policies to allow themselves to seize the time and celebrate [the] triumph of the Vietnamese people." The short statement hailed the victory as one shared by all enemies of US imperialism.[18]

●●●

Life in the underground, while never comfortable, had by now become familiar. Finances were still precarious, dependent on donations from sympathetic radicals and friends and on odd jobs. Bill Ayers later said that they "lived like hippies."[19] The development of bonds beyond politics, as discussed in "New Morning," continued in a natural way – as it would among any group of people sharing a daily life. Jane Alpert, who was still wanted (along with Pat Swinton) for the bombings of corporate offices in New York in November 1969, met up with some Weather people in 1972. Her account of these meetings give a flavour of their lives at this time. Her first encounter was with Mark Rudd who by this time was living apart from the group as Tony Schwartz, but remained in contact with them. Their meeting was the result of a chance encounter at a lecture they both attended in Santa Fe. After a short conversation there, they agreed to meet again the next day. While talking in a car near a park the following evening, a policeman approached them and asked for identification. They gave him their false papers, and the officer apologized for bothering them and returned to his car. Rudd told Alpert that he was living with a girlfriend from his college days who was not underground and that he was working off the books for a local construction firm.[20]

Alpert's next visit was with Bernardine Dohrn in San Francisco. After making arrangements over the phone, the two met in Golden Gate Park. During their conversation,

Dohrn mentioned that some Weather members were working for McGovern because of his promise to end the war immediately if elected. She also revealed that Rudd had been asked to leave the organization for a short time at the request of some of the women. Later that day the two met again at a local restaurant, along with Cathy Wilkerson.

The following day, Dohrn and Alpert went to Mt. Tamalpais, north of San Francisco. Dohrn spoke about the expanding role of women in the group and mentioned that some members were lesbian and lived with other Weather women in an all-women's collective. When the two parted ways, Dohrn gave Alpert Kathy Boudin's address in Boston and, after Alpert returned to the East Coast, she visited Boudin and her housemates. Although she argued with them over feminism and the Left, Alpert was impressed by Weather's "unanimity, preserved somehow across a continent and in spite of the difficulties of covert communication." She further noted that, "Nothing was more important to them than staying together."[21]

• • •

In the interim between the Pentagon bombing and the next major Weather action in September 1973 Weather seems to have been occupied with searching for a way to continue its political work among the people in a changing political situation brought about by the apparent victory of the Vietnamese and an economic downturn resulting from Nixon's attempt to reduce inflation and weaken labor. The absence of public actions and statements led some police agencies to speculate that Weather had disbanded or, at the least, forsaken politics.

One important influence on Weather's move toward a post-Vietnam reality was Clayton van Lydegraf, a seasoned leftist in his sixties who had been expelled from both the Communist Party and PL for his ultra-leftism. He had met some Weather people in Seattle at the beginning of the 1970s but did not spend much time with the group until early 1973. Van Lydegraf began working with Weather in a support role, encouraging the study of Marxist-Leninist theory. His intent was to bring an understanding of working-class struggle to Weather in the hope of expanding its base of support beyond an aging youth counter-culture. This process would take several turns in the months to come as some Weather members argued for a move into the workplace to organize and others opposed it. The ultimate result was a change in direction for Weather, which was to be defined in their statement, *Prairie Fire: The Politics of Revolutionary Anti-Imperialism* (1974).

On December 2, 1972, the federal government issued new, revised versions of the 1970 Detroit indictments against members of Weather on charges of conspiracy to bomb police departments throughout the US. The new indictments named, besides the original suspects, four other Weather members, and dropped charges previously brought against the FBI informer Larry Grathwohl. The new Weather indictees were John Fuerst (a Columbia SDS member since 1966), Leonard Handelsman from Cleveland, Mark Real from Kent, and Roberta Smith from California. Besides the conspiracy charges from the first indictments, these new indictments also charged those named with transporting explosives across state lines and firebombing a Cleveland policeman's home on March 2, 1970. These indictments were later dropped on the grounds of illegality in break-ins and surveillance by FBI agents. In the first arrest of a Weather fugitive since 1971, police charged Howie Machtinger during the week of September 20, 1973. It is quite possible that information regarding his whereabouts was found in papers stolen from his brother's house in New York by FBI agents. Machtinger was one of Weather's original members and a co-author of the founding statement.

●●●

After several months of harassment and economic and political subversion, the September 11, 1973 coup in Chile served notice to the world that the United States, despite its failures in Indochina, had not changed. Indeed, the coup was a model rescue of multinational profits from a popular socialist government. With financial and propaganda assistance from ITT and Anaconda Copper – both corporations with large holdings in Chile – the US government made it virtually impossible for the elected Chilean government to function. By late summer 1973, a CIA-funded trucker's strike paralyzed the country. With the middle-class staging one-day strikes and shop closures, the socialist government found itself under siege. Its destruction was completed on September 11, when rightist military forces attacked the centers of government in Santiago, the capital city. Within a week, right-wing elements in the military controlled the country; thousands of citizens were dead, including President Allende, and thousands more imprisoned.

Although the world had been forewarned by a series of revelations about the subversion of the Chilean Left's electoral victory by the CIA and ITT, made public during the 1972 US presidential campaign, the US Left reacted angrily. On September 27, Weather attacked the New York offices of the Latin American division of ITT, adding its "voice to the international expression of outrage and anger at the involvement of ITT and the US government in the overthrow of socialist Chile." The presence of the bomb had been called in approximately 20 minutes before it exploded by a male who identified himself as a member of the Weather Underground and stated that the attack was in retaliation for ITT's crimes against the Chilean people. The explosion destroyed the furniture and walls in the ninth-floor reception area and sent five large window panels to the street below.

The communiqué accompanying the bombing described the process by which the socialist government had been destroyed. After briefly defining the dependent relationship of Chile and the United States, Weather explained the Chilean popular movement's reclamation of the people's wealth through nationalization and land redistribution. Noting the history of popular Left governments in Latin America, and Chile's increasingly important role in the Latin American revolutionary process prior to the coup, Weather said it had just been a matter of time before the United States would end the government's rule. ITT and Anaconda were natural allies in that project. Part of their strategy involved forcing a drop in international copper prices, something Anaconda could afford, given its worldwide domination of the market. Chile, however, suffered from the price drop. When this was combined with other elements of the US blockade, the United States and its right-wing allies in Chile had only to wait until economic crisis brought about the government's fall. Weather's statement ended hopefully, nonetheless, encouraging US leftists to acquaint themselves with the writings of Latin American revolutionaries and poets and to challenge ITT and other multinationals everywhere.[22]

Finally, many members of the SLA are still free. They must be defended, publicly and privately. Anyone who is in a position to help them directly should give them encouragement, support, shelter, and love. Empty your pockets. Struggle with them. Learn from them. We must protect our fighters.

Weather communiqué, May 24, 1974[23]

Domestically, the arrival of the Symbionese Liberation Army and Federation (SLA) provided Weather with the possibility of allies in the armed struggle. Except for the Black Liberation Army (BLA), an offshoot of the New York Panthers, and the George Jackson Brigade in the Pacific northwest, Weather had been pretty much alone in its continued insistence on the need for armed struggle in the United States. The SLA, however, like Weather, was a clandestine army without a political wing. Its first communiqué, in late August 1973, was a declaration of war against the "Fascist capitalist class and all their agents of murder, oppression, and exploitation." The rest of the document listed the specific goals of the organization and detailed its structure. The most important aspects of SLA, as far as its future went, were its multiracial composition and its top-heavy hierarchical structure. Many on the Left would later cite that hierarchy as evidence of police involvement in the organization.

The actions of the SLA, especially the kidnapping of newspaper heiress Patricia Hearst in February 1974, provoked a paranoid reaction among the Left, already unduly suspicious because of the fear-ridden climate prevalent at the time, itself in large part resulting from the publication in the mainstream press of details of the state's counter-intelligence activities against the Left. These revelations were part of the flood of disclosures regarding government illegalities unleashed in the wake of the Watergate breakin. Even the minimal knowledge of law-enforcement tactics learned from the press encouraged the Left in its collective fear to visualize police agents behind every unfamiliar group and action. However, one unlikely result of these revelations was the complete dismissal of charges against the twelve Weather members of conspiracy in the Days of Rage indictments. On January 3, 1974, Judge Hoffman threw out the case because he believed the government's action had no substance once the illegally obtained evidence was removed.

The Panthers conducted their own investigation of the SLA, which convinced them that Donald DeFreeze, the SLA "commander," was indeed a police agent.[24] Whether or not the SLA was infiltrated by police, or even created by them, Weather assumed it was not and, in a communiqué dated February 20, 1974, praised the Hearst kidnapping, which "unleashed an astounding practical unity among people's organizations."[25] These so-called "people's organizations" were the two or three other ultra-Left organizations also involved in guerrilla activities, primarily bombings.

The Weather statement spoke positively of the SLA's ransom demand to William Hearst – the distribution of several million dollars worth of food to the poor of Oakland and San Francisco – and condemned the hunger experienced by those people as a "secret form of murder," just another kind of violence perpetrated against third-world people in the United States, comparing it to more obvious types such as police murders and harassment. According to Weather, the SLA action and its accompanying demands showed Americans that they could not ignore the violence of a system in which one man's riches kept others hungry.

Furthermore, the statement attacked the tendency of the

Left to disassociate itself from so-called extremists. Recalling earlier days, when even draft-card burning was dismissed as extremist, Weather warned its readers not to "do the enemy's work by asserting their own moderation and legitimacy." With a touch of irony, the statement noted that, since the arrival of the SLA, Weather had been touted as a "moderate alternative" by the establishment press. That characterization, according to Weather, exposed a racist bias because the SLA was multiracial and Weather was not. The organization called on the Left to keep in the forefront of its collective mind the primary issues of "official violence and repression" raised by the SLA, and reminded fellow revolutionaries that Nat Turner and John Brown were attacked as lunatics in their time. It was only in retrospect, the statement continued, that revolution was officially revered. In short, Weather urged the revolutionary Left to support the SLA.[26]

By now, Weather's numbers were small. A committed core of perhaps fifty individuals divided into small units moved about the country and occasionally took some kind of political action. Judging from the location of these acts, the primary cells or "families" were located in the San Francisco Bay Area and somewhere in the northeast. On March 7, 1974 – the day before International Women's Day and the day after the fourth anniversary of the death of Robbins, Oughton, and Gold in the townhouse explosion – the Women's Brigade placed a bomb in the San Francisco offices of the Department of Health, Education, and Welfare. This was the Women's Brigade's first public action since October 1970 (when, as the Proud Eagle Tribe, they had exploded a bomb at Harvard). The explosion was small and caused little damage other than some charred walls and shattered windows.

The accompanying statement addressed further the issues of hunger and poverty raised by the SLA kidnapping of Hearst. Insisting that the welfare system was a counter-insurgency program against women, especially those of color, Weather compared being on welfare to "having a sexist tyrant for an old man . . . You give up control of your bodies and most of your dignity as a condition of aid; he controls your money and your privacy."[27] This analysis, however, did not lead Weather to join or endorse struggles demanding day-care and welfare rights. Instead, the belief that any reforms merely extended the rule of the imperialist class prevailed. By maintaining that perspective, Weather went against the trend on the Left toward organizing around bread-and-butter issues and marginalized itself by insisting that any reforms short of revolution "became their opposite when they remained in the hands of the ruling class," even if those activities could be partially controlled by the community.[28]

• • •

Apparent in all Weather statements after 1972 is a decrease in counter-culture rhetoric. Implicit in this change was a tacit acknowledgement of the system's successful cooptation of most of the counter-culture's non-political trappings. That cooptation provided the youth of the 1970s with an apolitical culture of sex, drugs, and rock-and-roll. This isn't to say that youth no longer thought in political terms, but the absence of the draft, the fragmention of the anti-war movement, and the McGovern campaign of 1972, combined to convince white youth that they were no longer politically threatened by the state as a group unless they chose to be. With the exception of a few radical communities and newspapers, the culture assumed a predominantly ultra-liberal content which, at best, preached cultural and personal freedom and political cynicism.

Weather continued its intense self-criticism in an attempt to adapt to the changing US political situation. As the victory of the Vietnamese continued to consolidate, the Left in the United States did the opposite. The SLA, BLA, and other clandestine, militarily inclined groups intensified their guerrilla campaigns at the same time as anti-Marxist-Leninist elements continued their rightward move into the Democratic Party. The Panthers, Young Lords, and other community-orientated groups (such as Rising Up Angry[29]) stepped up their community efforts, including running and supporting candidates in local elections. Many other organizations, the Revolutionary Union among them, focused on the deepening economic crisis of capitalism after the Vietnam war. These groups gave most of their efforts to organizing white workers in the workplace around layoffs and cutbacks. Once again, the question of racism in the United States had to be confronted. Some organizations, when faced with racist attitudes among white workers, chose to ignore them, concentrating instead on workplace issues which sidestepped race.

Support for workplace issues surfaced in Weather too, but because of its emphatic insistence on destroying racism wherever it appeared, the group's support of union struggles was limited. The statement accompanying the bombing of the Health, Education, and Welfare building on March 7, 1974 expressed continuing concern over racism and challenged the trend in the feminist movement to place personal liberation above the liberation of all women.[30] The Weather statement urged feminists to see women's liberation as a matter of survival, not just expression. Something poor women knew only too well was that "food, decent medical care, good schools and community run day-care" were essential to their liberation, not only from poverty, but in their struggle to achieve personal freedoms as well. Weather accused white feminists of pursuing their own desires under the veil of feminism and not including survival issues in their agenda.

● ● ●

The saga of the SLA took a televised turn for the worse in the weeks that followed the Hearst kidnapping. For one, Patty Hearst joined the group, taking the revolutionary name of Tania – after Che Guevara's companion. The organization left its Berkeley base and headed south where, after robbing a bank and a sporting-goods store, it finally holed up in a house in the Compton section of Los Angeles. Within days of their arrival in Compton, the police located them and, on May 4, surrounded the house with over 500 agents. The officers proceeded to attack the occupants with automatic weapons fire and gas. Six members of the SLA died. After several hours of televised battle, the surviving members surrendered. A Weather statement given to the press on May 24 hailed the SLA for their revolutionary actions. It also criticized the Left's failure, once again, to perceive armed groups as allies and to support them. It was that failure, Weather implied, which was partially responsible for the SLA's tragic end.

NOTES

1. Panther 21, "Open Letter to Weatherman," *Eugene Augur*, Eugene, Oregon, January, 1971.
2. *Underground*, directed by Emilio DeAntonio, First Run Features, New York, 1976.
3. Select Committee to Study Governmental Operations with Regard to Intelligence Activities, p. 205.
4. From a leaflet distributed at Vietnam Veterans Against the War encampment, April 1971.
5. Staff, "Mayday Issue," *Quicksilver Times*, Washington, D.C., May 14, 1971.
6. Weatherman, "Letter to Moms Everywhere," *Quicksilver Times*, Washington, D.C., June 2, 1971, p. 5.
7. Bettina Aptheker, "Social Functions of Prison in the United States," *If They Come in the Morning*, Signet, New York, 1971, p. 57.
8. Staff, "George Jackson," *Berkeley Tribe*, Berkeley, Cal., August 27, 1971, p. 2.
9. Weather Underground, "Tribute to George Jackson," *Georgia Straight*, Atlanta, Ga., August 31, 1971, p. 2.
10. Ibid.
11. Attica Liberation Front, quoted in Tom Wicker, *A Time to Die*, New York Times Book Co., New York, 1975, p. 315.
12. Wicker, *A Time to Die*, p. 278.
13. Weather Underground, Communiqué, quoted in *Vancouver Free Press*, Vancouver, September 28, 1971, p. 16.
14. Weather Underground, "Today, We Attacked the Pentagon," *Liberated Guardian*, New York, June 1972.
15. Anonymous, "Eyewitness Account," *Quicksilver Times*, Washington, D.C., May 31, 1972.
16. The author's recollection.
17. "Today, We Attacked the Pentagon."
18. Weather Underground, "Common Victories," quoted in a leaflet distributed at an anti-war rally, Winter 1973.
19. Telephone conversation with Ayers, November 11, 1996.
20. Jane Alpert, *Growing Up Underground*, Morrow, New York, 1981, p. 322.
21. Ibid., pp. 332–3. In 1973, Alpert wrote an open "Letter to the underground" in which she renounced her leftist past in favor of what she termed radical feminism. She had been friends with Robin Morgan for years, and Morgan helped her write the letter. She attacked the male members of Weather and, intentionally or not, provided leads for law-enforcement agents still looking for Weather fugitives. In her memoir *Growing Up Underground*, she recanted many of her remarks in that letter.
22. Weather Underground, "Communique 14," *City Star*, New York, September 27, 1973.
23. Weather Underground Organization, "Weather Letter," *City Star*, May 24, 1974.
24. A series of articles in the *Black Panther* appeared over the spring and summer of 1974 detailing "leader" Donald DeFreeze's [Cinque's] dealings with various police agencies. He was familiar to Los Angeles Panthers from the late

1960s, when he worked with Louis Tackwood of the Los Angeles Police Department Criminal Conspiracy Section. In 1970, while in Vacaville Prison Facility, he was also recruited by the CIA and the California Attorney General's office. His work involved establishing a project known as UNISIGHT, designed to attract white radicals in the prison movement and keep an eye on them. In December 1972, DeFreeze was moved to Soledad prison where, after a couple of months, he was transferred to a minimum-security wing of the prison reserved for trusted inmates and informers. It was from this wing that DeFreeze walked away from the "escape-proof" prison and headed for the Bay Area.

25.   Weather Underground, "A Massive Morality Play . . .", February 20, 1974.

26.   Ibid.

27.   Women's Brigade, Weather Underground, "The Department of Health, Education, and Welfare Is an Enemy of Women," March 1974.

28.   Ibid.

29.   Rising Up Angry were multiracial revolutionary youth organizations formed among working-class youth in Southern California and Chicago by some former members of RYM II.

30.   Women's Brigade, "Health, Education, and Welfare Is an Enemy of Women."

7...

A Second Wind? The **Prairie Fire** Statement

We are a guerrilla organization. We are communist women and men, underground in the United States for more than four years. We are deeply affected by the historic events of our time in the struggle against U.S. imperialism.

Our intention is to disrupt the empire, to incapacitate it, to put pressure on the cracks, to make it hard to carry out its bloody functioning against the people of the world, to join the world struggle, to attack from the inside.

Our intention is to engage the enemy, to wear away at him, to isolate him, to expose every weakness, to pounce, to reveal his vulnerability.

Our intention is to encourage the people, to provoke leaps in confidence and consciousness, to stir the imagination, to popularize power, to agitate, to

> *organize, to join in every possible way the people's day*
> *to day struggles.*
>
> *Our intention is to forge an underground, a*
> *clandestine political organization engaged in every*
> *form of struggle, protected from the eyes and weapons*
> *of the state, a base against repression, to accumulate*
> *lessons, experience and constant practice, a base from*
> *which to attack.*
>
> *Opening statement of Prairie Fire[1]*

Weather staged some armed actions in 1974, including its final bombing of the year on June 13 of Gulf Oil's headquarters in Pittsburgh – an act in solidarity with the anti-colonial struggle against Portugal in Angola which caused over $350,000 worth of damage. But the group's major achievement of the year was not any armed action, or its statements concerning the SLA; it was the release in midsummer of *Prairie Fire: The Politics of Revolutionary Anti-Imperialism.* This 188-page work was the product of more than twelve months of thought, discussion, writing, and rewriting. The first detailed statement of Weather's politics since "You Don't Need a Weatherman" in June 1969, it described the group's plans for the immediate future and, like the "New Morning" statement, included criticism of its past. Most of the book consists of a summary of Weather history and a leftist history of the United States.

The book was rewritten four times in the course of a year before it was collectively adopted by the organization and published. Most of the writing was done by Bernardine Dohrn, Bill Ayers, Jeff Jones, and Celia Sojourn (a pseudonym for several unnamed individuals). After each draft,

The "letterhead" of the New Morning statement, from the
collection of Will Miller, reproduced courtesy of *Liberated Guardian*
(top); and the logo of the Prairie Fire Organizing Committee,
from the PFOC collection, reproduced courtesy of the staff of
Breakthrough.

copies were relayed to the remaining Weather "families" for discussion and revision. Van Lydegraf was also sent one of the later drafts for his input and it was his press which printed the final version. The distribution was coordinated by van Lydegraf, Jennifer Dohrn, and a number of other activists who formed the Prairie Fire Distributing Committee. The first edition appeared in bookstores in San Francisco, Berkeley, Chicago, Madison, New York, and elsewhere throughout the United States on July 24, 1974. Eventually over 40,000 copies were distributed.

On the assumption that "the unique and fundamental condition of this time is the decline of US imperialism," Weather challenged the anti-imperialist movement to continue its revolutionary path. The group renounced its previous tendency which demanded an immediate revolution in the United States and declared that an American revolution would be "complicated and protracted" and involve many forms of struggle, armed and not. The years of political work, individually and collectively, undertaken by Weather enabled its members to place the struggle in a perspective they did not have in 1969. While maintaining Weather's internationalist context, *Prairie Fire* urged patience and warned against some "magical moment of insurrection." Reflecting a consciousness developed over years of revolutionary work, clandestine and aboveground, Weather urged revolutionaries in the US to organize and prepare constantly wherever they were and in whatever way possible.

Prairie Fire represented a shift in strategy, but one which had been developing since "New Morning, Changing Weather." While that statement had recognized the need for an underground army not to isolate itself from the masses, it was criticized for minimalizing the role of armed actions.

Prairie Fire attempted to reconcile this apparent dichotomy by repeatedly emphasizing the importance of mass revolutionary organizing, while describing Weather as an underground organization. What this suggested was that Weather saw itself as the beginnings of a revolutionary people's army aligned with the revolutionary movement. This differed from their previous self-perception as primarily a foco organization whose role was to commit armed actions without any concern for organizing a political movement to support those acts. Whether or not the rest of the revolutionary movement shared Weather's new perception of itself was questionable, primarily because most revolutionary groups of the period were in the process of either reorganization or disintegration. Those revolutionaries not in organizations, meanwhile, were hesitant to align themselves with any group and often unwilling to even speak in terms of revolution, given the paranoia and lack of direction in the movement at the time.

This widely felt disillusionment in the movement was the result of multiple factors. Foremost among these were the counter-insurgency efforts of the state. Although the intensity of the legal and illegal campaign against the anti-war and anti-racist movements had decreased somewhat by 1974, the effects of COINTELPRO were still felt. Other factors which contributed to the despair of the Left in the 1970s, in Weather's opinion, concerned tendencies within the movement itself – including a distrust of organizations, cynicism, racism, and sexism.

According to *Prairie Fire*, distrust of organizations arose from their failures, and the trend in organizations to replicate the hierarchical structures of the dominant society. In its early months, Weather was itself guilty of this. However, as the organization matured, the tendency to mimic the sexist structure of, and manipulate differences prevalent in, capitalist society eventually diminished. Distrust of movements was also evident in a turn toward cynicism in the early 1970s. From *National Lampoon*'s satirical portraits of the anti-war movement to the distrustful mood expressed in rock music (for example, Lennon/Ono's "The Dream Is Over"), the general tendency among young people during this period was to abandon all hope. Weather sympathized with the demoralization and sense of hopelessness felt by many activists and blamed much of the prevailing attitude on the cult of individualism in US society. *Prairie Fire* encouraged understanding and urged the Left to persist in the struggle, especially in fighting sexism and racism in society and the movement. These struggles were critical as activists now organized more in the workplace, where racist and sexist unions and union members were commonly found.

Turning from the Left to the world situation, *Prairie Fire* warned that "conditions will not wait." The statement then proceeded to analyze two crises in the US in 1974. The first was Watergate. Calling it a "magnificent victory of the struggles of the Sixties," Weather recognized the troubles of the Nixon regime as a "reflection of the US empire in crisis" and a battle for power among the ruling elites. For Weather, the actual breakin at the Watergate Hotel was a logical extension of the Nixon program of militarization; *Prairie Fire* discussed the prosecution of the case and noted that all "the Watergate investigations . . . never explored Nixon's deliberate aggression against Black, Chicano, and Puerto Rican communities," nor the criminal actions undertaken in Indochina. Nonetheless, in Weather's opinion the crisis was a victory for the people because it destroyed "the myth of American freedom and democracy."

The imperial myth described by Weather was further undermined by the advent of the energy crisis of 1973 – a crisis which, according to Weather, was "*the* crisis of imperialism." In an attempt to maintain their rate of profit in the face of the formation of the oil cartel (OPEC), the energy companies, along with the government, devised a phony oil shortage, providing them with an excuse to more than double prices and thereby maintain their already high profits. In turn, these profits enabled corporations to buy out smaller companies and consolidate their monopoly. Then, according to Weather, while American drivers sat in lines to buy overpriced gasoline, the Navy consumed over one-third of the oil used by the US.

Weather pointed out that this "crisis of imperialism" was evident in the ecological devastation caused by the continual exploitation of the earth by big business, and in the use of energy cost increases as reasons to refuse labor demands. It was further evident in the high food prices brought about by increased transportation costs to agribusiness, and in the rent increases charged by landlords to cover their costs.

Above all, *Prairie Fire* was a call to organize. Weather asked questions that all revolutionary movements throughout history had faced, and sought to apply the lessons it had learned to a program for the US revolution in the 1970s. Once again identifying US imperialism as the enemy of the world's peoples, Weather stated that its goal was to "attack imperialism's ability to exploit and wage war," and to eventually build a socialist society in the United States. To begin this process, Weather reiterated its original thesis that the empire must be at least partially destroyed. Naturally, the weakest links in the imperialist chain were the colonies. For that reason, claimed Weather (as it always had), it was the liberation of the third world which held the key to the eventual liberation of the mother country.

To assist in the liberation of the colonies, the Left in the United States needed organization. Without organization, Weather insisted, there could be only limited direction or results in political work. In a statement indicative of the political understanding gained from Weather's experiences, *Prairie Fire* urged people to never "dissociate mass struggle from revolutionary violence." To do so, claimed Weather, was to do the state's work. Just as in 1969–70, Weather still refused to renounce revolutionary violence for "to leave people unprepared to fight the state is to seriously mislead them about the inevitable nature of what lies ahead." It was Weather's belief that imperialism would not "decay peacefully."

The difference in Weather's insistence on the need for revolutionary violence in 1969–70 and in 1974 concerned the role of the mass movement. In 1969, after the failure of the Days of Rage to involve thousands of youth in massive street fighting, Weather renounced most of the Left and decided to operate as an isolated underground group. That decision caused the group to lose sight of its commitment to mass struggle and made future alliances with the mass movement difficult and tenuous. By 1974, Weather had recognized this shortcoming and in *Prairie Fire* detailed a different strategy for the 1970s which demanded both mass and clandestine organizations. The role of the clandestine organization would be to build the "consciousness of action" and prepare the way for the development of a people's militia. Concurrently, the role of the mass movement would include support for, and encouragement of, armed action. Such an alliance would, according to Weather, "help create the 'sea' for the guerrillas to swim in."

The importance of revolutionary culture expressed by Weather in "New Morning" was addressed in various ways throughout *Prairie Fire*. While critical of the prevalent hedonistic tendencies of the youth culture, Weather hailed the communities the culture had built and urged them not to rest on their past achievements, but to continue their opposition to imperialist war, racism, and sexism. *Prairie Fire* insisted that revolutionaries needed to view the youth culture not as a thing of the past, but as a very real culture of opposition which could become permanent.

One method proposed by Weather to make it permanent was the proletarianization of the culture. While nominally defined as a consciousness of anti-imperialism, what Weather actually meant by "proletarianization," was identification with the populations of those nations victimized by imperialism and "discarding the privileges of empire." This definition, when placed in the context of Weather's internationalist worldview, where all oppressed people suffered at the hands of US imperialism, lent a new meaning to the concept.

The most striking differences in the analyses of "You Don't Need a Weatherman" and *Prairie Fire* lie in Weather's changing ideas regarding women and feminism. In sharp contrast to a professed ignorance of the women question in the earlier statement, *Prairie Fire* provided the reader with a clear analysis of the issue. Fundamental to its analysis was the belief that imperialism, by definition, necessitates the subjugation of women. As mentioned before, this change in awareness was related to the changing role of women in the organization and to certain trends as the women's movement grew in the early 1970s. One trend emphasized the advancement of individual women within the system; another insisted on a complete separation from men; and another saw the enemy not as men, but as the system of imperialism, which manipulated both sexism and racism to its own ends. It was this third trend which was both embraced and developed by Weather, along with other anti-imperialist groups and individuals.

This analysis implied an understanding that any improvements in the lives of women such as daycare, birth control, or even higher wages, were merely reforms and did not accomplish any fundamental change in women's lives or in the manner in which women were perceived. In fact, as stated in *Prairie Fire*, such reforms only made women's lives bearable and, consequently, showed both women and men that sexism would exist as long as imperialism did. *Prairie Fire*, echoing the Women's Brigade communiqué of March 7, 1974, argued that without the power to control daycare, birth control, and other aspects of their daily lives, women would find that any progressive reforms could and would "become their opposite in the hands of the ruling class." For example, birth control could become population control and daycare could be used for state indoctrination. For these reasons, then, Weather insisted, women must support socialist revolution and the revolution must support the women's movement.

The section on women attacked the racist tendencies within the women's movement and pointed to how the mainstream media had manipulated a fear of rape into a fear of third-world men. Weather challenged the complacency of much of the white feminist movement, and called for international solidarity with the women of the world, especially those in Vietnam, Palestine, and Puerto Rico.

To express that solidarity, and simultaneously express a "righteous anger at oppression," the statement encouraged women's resistance to sexism to be militant and courageous. To be otherwise, it argued, would detract from the history of women's resistance as well as imply acceptance of the violence of imperialism. In reply to those critics who considered militancy a macho or male response, Weather urged women to fight for the revolution as one lives for the revolution. In other words, with a total commitment without regard for personal reward.

For the most part, *Prairie Fire* was received positively by the revolutionary Left. The despair felt by many activists as they searched for a strategy to deal with the "Vietnamized" war in Indochina, which was still unresolved, and with the energy crisis and the economic recession, was lifted somewhat by the public release of the statement. At a press conference called by aboveground supporters and friends of Weather, a variety of activists spoke about it.

First, Jennifer Dohrn summarized the book's contents and placed the statement in the context of the period. It was, according to Dohrn, a period of reorganization and reflection for the American Left, and Weather's analysis could only enhance discussion about the future. Two other women present – Laura Whitehorn, a Weather supporter, and Ro Reilly, a Catholic anti-war activist – spoke of the statement's inclusiveness and understanding of women's needs and oppression. Whitehorn argued that *Prairie Fire* was "an articulation of true feminist politics set in the context of world forces" and urged revolutionary women to study the document. Red Murphy, a former Attica inmate, articulated the sentiments of those present when he said that *Prairie Fire*'s most important point was "its call for unity on the Left."[2]

In their review of *Prairie Fire*, the staff of *Takeover* in Madison, Wisconsin (by 1974, one of the few underground newspapers still holding true to its revolutionary roots), noted that the lack of "apocalyptic rage and rhetoric" in the book did not mean an end to Weather's militancy. Instead, argued the *Takeover* staff, the document "clari(fied) the present thinking of SDS's boldest heirs and spelled out the priorities of the seventies."[3]

As for some of SDS's other heirs, their response was critical. Carl Davidson, still writing a column for the *Guardian* and a member of the Los Angeles based Marxist-Leninist-Maoist group, the October League, accused Weather of "repudiating the proletariat" and having a "bankrupt line."[4] His primary criticism, however, concerned Weather's view of the role of national liberation movements, both internationally and domestically. According to the Leninist model, the proletariat is the main revolutionary force, and national movements become its allies. According to Weather, however, the revolutionary national movements were proletarian revolutions in their own right against the world imperialist class, and provided the leadership in the worldwide anti-imperialist revolution. This view, argued Davidson, rendered a workers' party irrelevant and made socialist revolution impossible. For Davidson, Weather had learned nothing in its years underground except perhaps better public-relations methods.[5]

Davidson's opinions are indicative of the state of the US Left at the time. The major leftist organizations of the late 1960s were, with the possible exception of Weather and the SWP, virtually non-existent. They were replaced nationally, during a period of open sectarianism and police provocation, with such organizations as the social-democratic New American Movement, the Marxist-Leninist-Maoist October League and Revolutionary Unions, and the increasingly isolated and reactionary Lyndon LaRouche front groups such as the Labor Committees and National Labor Party. The total membership of all these groups was microscopic in comparison to the movement's heyday – perhaps 3,000 at most. Other groups, such as the SLA, the New World Liberation Front (NWLF), the BLA, and similar clandestine organizations engaged in armed struggle, accounted for perhaps a couple of hundred more activists. What these numbers suggest is that the signing of the Vietnam peace accords, an increasing cynicism among youth, a growing awareness of the limitations of a culture based on youth and leisure, and the effectiveness of the government's counter-insurgency efforts insured that ever smaller numbers of American activists were committed to revolution.

NOTES

1.   All quotations in this chapter, unless otherwise noted, are from Weather Underground Organization, *Prairie Fire: The Politics of Revolutionary Anti-Imperialism*, Communications Co., 1974.

2.   Rosenstein, "Weather Manifesto Surfaces," *City Star*, September 1974.

3.   Staff, "A Single Spark Can Ignite a Prairie Fire", *Takeover*, September 9, 1974.

4.   The October League was formed in 1973 by members of a Los Angeles Marxist-Leninist cell and other communists. Davidson and Mike Klonsky were its best-known members. Their all-out support of China alienated them from much of the Left, especially their support of China's arming the Shah of Iran and other counter-revolutionary governments and movements (UNITA in Angola , for one).

5.   Carl Davidson, "Which Side Are You On?," *Guardian*, October 9, 1974.

8...

The End of the Tunnel: Weather and Its Successors

After the release of *Prairie Fire: The Politics of Revolutionary Anti-Imperialism*, Weather began actively building an aboveground support group named, appropriately, the Prairie Fire Organizing Committee (PFOC). The first chapters were formed in San Francisco, Los Angeles, New York, Boston, Seattle, and Chicago. In addition, a film, *Underground*, was made, a newsletter, *Osawatomie*, published, and a meeting – the Hard Times conference – called to gather movement activists together around the issues and hopes expressed in *Prairie Fire*. Meanwhile, van Lydegraf formally joined the organization, forsaking his aboveground support activities and going underground.

On January 23, 1975, the Agency for International Development (USAID) office in the State Department building in Washington, D.C., and the offices of the Department of

Defense in Oakland were bombed. These attacks were coordinated between at least one East Coast and one West Coast unit. The explosions caused over $50,000 worth of damage, and no injuries were reported. In a statement released to the press, Weather expressed solidarity with the Vietnamese still fighting against the Thieu regime in Vietnam and demanded an immediate and complete withdrawal of all US forces and aid. Weather ended the communiqué demanding that the US honor the peace accords signed two years earlier to the day.

On June 16, 1975, Weather bombed the Banco de Ponce office in New York's Rockefeller Center, causing several thousand dollars worth of damage. A statement was sent to the Associated Press, the *New York Post*, and NBC television detailing the role of the bank's owners in causing the poverty that was endemic in Puerto Rico. In addition, Weather expressed its support for the cement workers' strike then taking place against a construction company partially owned by the bank. On October 10, 1975, it bombed the Kennecott Corporation's headquarters in Salt Lake City, Utah, in solidarity with the resistance to Chile's military government and in opposition to the Kennecott Corporation's involvement in the coup two years earlier. The explosion was preceded by a phone call from a Weather woman to the *Salt Lake Tribune*. The blast tore through a restroom in the building and caused damage amounting to about $50,000.

•••

The *Hard Times* moniker was chosen for the conference in Chicago because of the rapidly deteriorating economic situation in the United States in the mid-1970s. Organizing for the conference was primarily undertaken by the PFOC, the Puerto Rican Socialist Party, United Black Workers, Youth Against War and Fascism (YAWF), and CASA – an organization of Mexican and Chicano workers who were mostly from the southwestern United States. Dozens of other activist groups and individuals were also involved, ranging from the Gray Panthers to various union locals and other small leftist cells. In the alternative press, the meeting was promoted almost invariably as an attempt to address issues affecting "working and oppressed people in the US [who] are under assault."[1] The organizers hoped that race and gender issues would also be addressed.

At first, the conference seemed a success, with two to four thousand people attending the opening session on the evening of January 30, 1976. This session was set up as a people's tribunal, and speakers representing organizations as various as the Zimbabwe African National Union and a steelworkers' local addressed the effects of US imperialism in the wake of the Vietnam war. Discussion of domestic issues related to the economic downturn prevailed, but international struggles also made the agenda – especially the civil war in Angola and the NLF victory in Vietnam the previous May.

The following day's agenda opened with a speech by Jennifer Dohrn, who enumerated the hopes of the organizers: "First, we have the responsibility of educating each other . . . Secondly, we have to develop a program of demands for the working class as a whole in this period to fight the depression . . . Finally, we will need to develop a way to function nationally . . ."[2]

Participants then broke into workshops for discussions and planning. When they regrouped it was apparent that, although everyone was optimistic, it would be a while before

Dohrn's hopes for a national program and plan of action would be realized. The divergent agendas of the plethora of organizations in attendance made this the only definite conclusion of the day. If anything, the multitude of agendas reminded everyone just how difficult it would be to forge a movement for the 1970s now that the single unifying issue of direct US military involvement in the war in Vietnam was gone. This was especially true given the inexperience of most participants in organizing around workplace issues. Furthermore, the change in the American workplace from a predominantly white male environment to a multicultural one, where women comprised nearly 50 per cent of the workers, demanded a new analysis and approach – one which would take more than a weekend to devise.

That isn't to say that nothing was accomplished. In fact, plans were set in motion for a mass demonstration to take place in Philadelphia on July 4 of that bicentennial year. A workplace bill of rights was also drafted, though never formalized. Other demonstrations were also planned and expressions of solidarity drafted for various events and groups. The conference had brought together a large, diverse group of Left activists and a very honest attempt at dialogue and coordination was made. Most media reporting the event, from the Maoist *Guardian* to the anarchist *Takeover*, agreed that the conference was successful at least in this regard.

In other respects, however, it failed. After several hours of workshops and discussions, the majority of participants joined a non-white caucus in accusing the PFOC, and by default Weather, of racism and sexism in its politics. The caucus of 250 or so delegates argued that the PFOC's attempts to incorporate labor issues into the conference agenda caused it to forsake important issues of race and gender by subordinating these categories to labor. Other far Left organizations, most notably the Revolutionary Communist Party, (RCP, formed in 1975 from the Bay Area Revolutionary Union headed by Bob Avakian), had already gone the route the PFOC was now accused of embarking on. That decision had caused RCP members to excuse some actions by white workers in the name of worker solidarity (the most egregious of these acts were the racist attacks by white workers in Boston during the controversial attempt to enforce school bussing there in the years 1974-6).

Unlike the RCP, however, Weather/PFOC did not equate the working class with the white working class. In all of its statements before and after Hard Times, it emphasized the diverse racial and cultural makeup of US workers and the specific exploitation which occurred because of a person's race and gender. Where it differed from its past analyses and ran into intense criticism, though, was in reneging on its support for the notion that the black population of the United States was a separate nation in favor of an analysis which relegated black Americans to the status of merely superexploited workers. Additionally, the analysis put forth by the PFOC at Hard Times acknowledged women's exploitation as members of the workforce, but not their special exploitation due solely to gender. These analyses would eventually lead to Weather's demise.

• • •

After the Hard Times conference public statements from Weather were usually signed by the PFOC, indicating the organizational confusion within the group in the wake of the Hard Times meeting. The New York PFOC, also known as the Central Committee (including Ayers, Jones, Bernardine Dohrn, Boudin, Dave Gilbert), came under attack for the supposedly reformist politics presented at the conference. Within the year, the rift between the Central Committee and the Bay Area Revolutionary Committee (van Lydegraf, Judith Bissell, Marc Perry, Mike Justesen, all out of Seattle, and others) was unbroachable. The Central Committee was also accused of "abandoning revolutionary anti-imperialism," an accusation that hit hard in an organization which had based its philosophy on the exact concept. The Revolutionary Committee denounced their former comrades in a document "reminiscent of the worst rhetorical and psychological aberrations of the New Left."[3] Although many leftists suspected that government provocateurism played a part in the split, those close to the PFOC claimed it was the result of long-term political differences over the role of reforms in the revolutionary struggle. The Central Committee's romanticization of workers led them into uncritical support of bread-and-butter struggles at the expense of anti-racist, anti-sexist, and anti-imperialist issues.

By the end of 1976, the Bay Area Revolutionary Committee had become the Weather Underground Organization (WUO). Bill Ayers, Jeff Jones, Bernardine Dohrn, Kathy Boudin, Dave Gilbert, and the others in the Central Committee had either been expelled or had left of their own volition. Although the PFOC was still a support group for those who held the Weather mantle, it began asserting a separate identity. The first issue of its political journal, *Breakthrough*, was published in March 1977 and dealt exclusively with the split in the WUO – a split which by this time had brought the demise of one faction.[4] Virtually the entire issue was filled with the Revolutionary Committee's "Provisional

—BREAKTHROUGH—

vol. 1 no.1   March 1977

INSIDE:
Provisional Political Statement
(includes major section on women's
oppression and liberation)
and writings by
--Native American Warriors
--Assata Shakur

POLITICAL JOURNAL of PFOC

The front cover of the first issue of *Breakthrough*, March 1977.
From the PFOC collection, reproduced courtesy of the staff of
Breakthrough.

Political Statement." Besides dismissing the old leadership of Weather (the New York group) as opportunists, much of the statement is a reassertion of the themes of *Prairie Fire*, with a somewhat more refined analysis of women's oppression and male supremacy. After relating the history of women's oppression in American history and noting its various forms as dependent on class and race, the section on women concludes by calling male supremacy "one of the chief competitive structures the imperialists have used to maintain divisions within the working class." Furthermore, the Revolutionary Committee insisted, no revolution can succeed which "does not attack one of the strongest bulwarks of imperialism – women's oppression and male supremacy."[5]

A pamphlet published by the John Brown Book Club (a branch of the PFOC in Seattle) around the same time as the first issue of *Breakthrough* detailed further reasons for the split. The most telling article in this collection is the transcript of a tape-recorded message from Bernardine Dohrn in which she apologized for the post *Prairie Fire* politics of Weather, stating, "Immediately after the publication of *Prairie Fire*, the Central Committee went back on the anti-imperialist line of *Prairie Fire* and aggressively opposed it."[6] In an analysis reminiscent of Weather's early, Days of Rage period, Dohrn criticized the actions of the Central Committee (and herself) and equated its support of workplace organizing with the support of an "opportunist white supremacist analysis."[7]

According to Dohrn, she and the Central Committee had followed the "classic path of white so-called revolutionaries who sold out the revolution."[8] Such harsh self-criticism may have seemed appropriate at the time, but with hindsight a more accurate analysis would have to acknowledge the growing role on the Left of identity politics, which caused many leftists to grasp at dogmatic straws in retaliation against the more liberal and right-wing elements of identity-based movements. This in turn encouraged groups like the New York Weather cell (who were attempting to create a class analysis which incorporated the special circumstances created by national and gender-based oppression) to adopt a politics demanding that the revolution wait on some of the more reactionary elements in US society. Although actions after *Prairie Fire* were meant to rectify Weather's earlier contempt of white workers, this was done at the expense of its traditional support base (New Left, counter-culture, third world), which it alienated in exchange for minimal levels of support among white workers, class-conscious or otherwise.

● ● ●

The Revolutionary Committee maintained Weather's long-standing position that organizing around reforms was opportunist and counter-revolutionary. After the split, the organization returned to action. On February 3, 1977, it bombed the San Francisco Immigration and Naturalization Service (INS) office, causing little damage, but announcing to those who still cared that the politics of armed struggle was once again the politics of Weather. News coverage was minimal, and for the most part overshadowed by the bombing of a car owned by a lawyer prosecuting a man charged in connection with a bombing by the New World Liberation Front. The Weather communiqué accompanying the action stated that the bomb was set off at the INS office to protest its role in the oppression and exploitation of undocumented workers.

The decision to resume the military option was pushed forward by van Lydegraf. It is worth noting, however, that two undercover agents (one each from the FBI and the California Criminal Intelligence Division) were working with the group, and it has been suggested that they encouraged the group to choose the reactionary and high-profile California State Senator John Briggs's office as their next target.

Months after the film *Underground* was released, a grand jury issued subpoenas to the filmmakers and other Hollywood figures. No one cooperated in this belated and feeble attempt to ferret out the remaining Weather fugitives, and law-enforcement agents turned to other, more outlandish schemes. For example, they seriously considered kidnaping Jennifer Dohrn's baby in an attempt to persuade her sister Bernardine to surrender.[9] Although this particular plan never came to anything, the fact that it was considered at all illustrates the extremes the state was prepared to go to in order to crush Weather and the spirit of resistance it symbolized. Even after the size and importance of Weather had greatly diminished, surveillance continued, as is indicated by papers released later under the Freedom of Information Act and by the Senate Judiciary Subcommittee.

California State Senator John Briggs was the author of an initiative slated for the California ballot which would have made it illegal for gays and lesbians to teach in public schools. The initiative was opposed by civil libertarians, gay and lesbian rights organizations, most of the Democratic Party, and, indeed, most Californians. According to the undercover agents who had infiltrated Weather, the bombing of Briggs's offices was to be the first of a series of attacks on government buildings and assassinations of public officials. However, given the history of law-enforcement agencies in their dealings with Weather, that claim is entirely questionable. At any rate, five members of the WUO – van Lydegraf, Mike T. Justesen, Marc

Perry, Judith Bissell, and a woman originally identified as Esther (later discovered to be Grace Fortner) – were arrested in Houston and Los Angeles on November 20, 1977 in connection with the plot, and all were to serve two years in California state prisons. The arrests were a front-page story in the *Los Angeles Times*, which was continued on page 2 next to an article headlined, "FBI Took Credit for Black Panther Split, Files Show." The irony of this juxtaposition of articles is only too apparent, given the similar lines along which the Panthers and Weather split, and the fact that the offspring of both splits would soon come together.

● ● ●

A few weeks before the Briggs arrests, another Weather member made the news. Mark Rudd, a participant in the Columbia uprising and the Days of Rage, and one of the authors of the original Weather statement, turned himself in to the Manhattan District Attorney on charges stemming from the Columbia action. When asked by a photographer blocking his way as he entered the courthouse if he had anything to say, Rudd replied, "Yeh, can I please go in?" From New York, he headed to Chicago and answered the Days of Rage indictments. He was released on $4,000 bail. Underground since the Flint war council in December 1969, Rudd had decided to surface.[10] On January 20, 1978, the *New York Times* reported that he had pled guilty to two counts of aggravated battery and received a $2,000 fine and two years probation.

Rudd's surrender was one of several that occurred during 1977. Phoebe Hirsch, Robert Roth, and Peter Clapp, all living in Chicago at the time, also surrendered to police that year.

The surrender of Hirsch and Roth at the Cook County Courthouse on March 25 1977, led some government officials to speculate that all members of Weather would turn themselves in as part of a decision to organize openly and aboveground. This speculation proved wrong. Both Hirsch and Roth were released – she on a personal recognizance bond and he on $1,000 bail. On September 13, each pled guilty to mob-action charges and received $1,000 fines and two years probation. Clapp surrendered on June 21 in another Chicago courtroom. Despite the best efforts of FBI officials, none of the Weather members who surfaced that year provided law-enforcement officials with any information on his/her life underground or about the whereabouts of the other seventeen Weather fugitives. Two more surfaced on March 23, 1978: John Fuerst and Roberta Smith were both released on $50,000 bonds after turning themselves in on an indictment drawn up against them in 1971 and charging them with transporting explosives. Fuerst eventually pled guilty to lesser charges and received a $2,000 fine and two years probation. Charges against Smith were apparently dropped.

Like Rudd, the Weather members who turned themselves in during this period had not been publicly active for two or three years and were taking advantage of the healing political climate that President Jimmy Carter's partial amnesty for draft resisters seemed to herald. The story of Weather now divides into that of the various organizations it spawned.

• • •

The Briggs plot was the last act planned by Weather as an organization. Those who had split with the Revolutionary

Committee almost a year before the arrests continued their lives underground. Bernardine Dohrn and Bill Ayers lived in New York, where they worked a variety of jobs and raised their child. Jeff Jones also lived in the New York City area with Eleanor Raskin, working as a laborer and helping to raise their child while also maintaining contact with their friends in the underground. Kathy Boudin, Dave Gilbert, Linda Evans, and Judy Clark helped form the May 19 Communist Organization, named in honor of Malcolm X and Ho Chi Minh, who were both born on this date.

The May 19 Communist Organization was an offshoot of the New York PFOC. Their primary raison d'être lay in supporting the BLA. The PFOC, meanwhile, existed primarily on the West Coast, publishing *Breakthrough* and lending solidarity to third-world national liberation struggles in Palestine, Zaire, Angola, and Puerto Rico. In order to address the upsurge in right-wing paramilitary and political organizing, the John Brown Anti-Klan Committee (JBAKC) was formed in 1978. Also an offshoot of the PFOC, its stated purpose was to fight the racists in and out of uniform and to help "free the Black nation."[11] JBAKC's vocal and militant presence at neofascist rallies usually overshadowed that of more traditional anti-racist groups in the late 1970s and through the 1980s.

The East Coast based May 19 Organization, meanwhile, fought racism in its own way. Most noteworthy was its logistical assistance in the prison escape of BLA member Assata Shakur from the Clinton Correctional Institution for Women in New Jersey on November 2, 1979; she had been serving time for her presence at a 1973 shootout with police which ended in the death of an officer.[12] The May 19 Organization also joined others at various actions in support of Puerto Rican *independentistas* and in opposition to international racism (especially during the tour of the official South African rugby team).

The participation of the PFOC, the JBAKC, and the May 19 Organization in public events into the 1990s enabled those individuals and organizations in the movement who were so inclined to take a more militant approach than that being urged by the mainstream groups. For example, during a protest in San Francisco on April 16, 1984, against Henry Kissinger's speech to the Foreign Policy Association and US involvement in Central America, it was the PFOC who encouraged demonstrators to move outside the limits agreed by police and marshals and, by doing so, raised the question of US involvement in the region with a wider public via the evening news. The crowd swelled to over a thousand, and the police attacked, swinging clubs and arresting dozens. In the news reports which followed, the PFOC and the Revolutionary Communist Party were specifically mentioned by police and media as the groups responsible for the police reaction. At a demonstration a week or two later, when El Salvadorean president Duarte spoke at the same hotel, the PFOC responded to the charges leveled against it with a leaflet titled "It's Right to Resist." Despite attempts to isolate the PFOC from the mainstream by blaming it for the police attacks, the opposite occurred. At the Duarte demonstration, even more protestors were willing to support those who crossed police lines.

● ● ●

The Weather members who had not joined the May 19 Organization or stayed with the PFOC began to appear aboveground in the early 1980s. Cathy Wilkerson was the first of the old leadership to surface after Mark Rudd had led the way. On July 8, 1980, she read a statement to reporters which gave her reasons for surrendering as personal, yet insisted that neither her beliefs nor commitment to changing the social and political conditions in America had altered. When asked where she had been living since the townhouse explosion she refused to say. She was released on $10,000 bail for charges related to that explosion ten years earlier and was eventually sentenced to three years in prison.[13]

On December 3, 1980, Bernardine Dohrn and Bill Ayers surfaced in New York. Rumors of the surrender had been in the New York press for several days and, when the couple at last appeared, the media were out in force. They both gave brief statements. Dohrn refused to recant her past, and flew to Chicago to face the remaining charges there. All charges against Ayers had been dropped earlier, but Dohrn received three years probation and a $1,500 fine.

Dohrn and Ayers had been living as Lou Douglas and Anthony Lee on West 123rd Street in Manhattan with their two children. This was at least their second address since moving to New York in the 1970s. Bernardine was working as a waitress at Teacher's restaurant on Broadway and 82nd Street, and Ayers worked at a daycare center. At the sentencing, the judge admonished Dohrn: "We have a system for change that does not involve violence," he said. Dohrn replied that she and the judge "had differing views on America."[14]

Less than a year later, in October 1981, Jeff Jones was arrested in the Bronx while he watched the World Series with his partner Eleanor Raskin. He had been using the name John Maynard, and Raskin had been living as his wife Sally. Both were wanted on charges related to a cache of explosives discovered by police in New Jersey in 1979. At the time of the Jones/Raskin arrest police assumed there was a connection between the couple and those arrested in the failed Brinks holdup attempt in Nyack, New York, which had occurred a few days earlier. There was none. Jones ended up on a year's probation for charges from 1970, and Raskin's charges were dismissed.

The Brinks holdup attempt hit the news on October 20, 1981. In what was to have been an expropriation of monies to finance the work of the BLA, Kathy Boudin, Dave Gilbert, Judy Clark, and BLA member Sam Brown were arrested while attempting to rob a Brinks armored truck operating in suburban New York. Two policemen were killed. Two days later Mtayari Sundiata of the BLA was also killed in a shootout with police and another BLA member was arrested. This act marked the end of that part of the underground Left formed in the anti-racist and anti-war struggles of the 1960s and 1970s. As far as those arrested were concerned, they would probably spend most of the rest of their lives in prison. After a long series of trials, during which Dohrn and Ayers took care of Boudin and Gilbert's child, Gilbert, Clark, and Boudin were found guilty of robbery and murder. Dohrn also spent seven months in prison for refusing to talk to a grand jury about the case. Those BLA members who were captured by police were also eventually found guilty and sentenced to long terms in prison.

In January, 1983, Linda Evans and other activists involved in the PFOC, May 19, and other similar organizations formed the Armed Resistance Unit. The group began a series of attacks on military and corporate targets which culminated in the bombing of the US Capitol on November 7, 1983, after the invasion of Grenada. A couple of years later, Evans and two other women – Marilyn J. Buck and Laura Whitehorn – were arrested in Baltimore, Maryland. By that time several other members of the Armed Resistance Unit were already serving long prison terms. Evans was sentenced to forty years.

After Evans's arrest, the Justice Department announced that there was only one Federal Weather fugitive left: Silas Bissell, who had jumped bail after he and his ex-wife were arrested for an attempted bombing of the ROTC building at the University of Washington in 1970. In 1987, Bissell was found living near Eugene, Oregon, as Terry Jackson and was arrested, tried, and sentenced, serving two years in a Federal prison.

During the US war against Iraq in 1990–91, certain former Weather members made the news once again, notably Bill Ayers, who helped to organize the opposition to the war in the Chicago area, where he now teaches. The PFOC was prominent in both San Francisco and Seattle, leading and helping to organize the more militant direct actions, including a shutdown of the Oakland Bay Bridge.

On January 6, 1994, one of the last of those charged in the Days of Rage went to court. Twenty-five years after the first national Weather action, Jeff Powell ended his life underground to face riot charges. He was fined $500 and placed on probation. Nearly a quarter-century after Weather called on the youth of America to bring the war home, Powell, a foot soldier in the Days of Rage, finally surrendered.[15]

NOTES

1.   S. Shelton , "Hard Times to Focus on Fight for Jobs," *Worker's World*, New York, January 30, 1976, p. 3.

2.   Irwin Silber, "Hard Times at Chicago Meeting," *Guardian*, February 1, 1976, p. 1.

3.   Peter Biskind, "Weather Underground Splits on Whether to Go Overground," *SevenDays*, Institute for New Communications, Farmington, N.Y., February 28, 1977, p. 17.

4.   *Breakthrough* ceased publication in the early part of the 1990s. However, at the time of writing, plans are under way to publish the journal in a different, less expensive format – probably on the World Wide Web.

5.   Revolutionary Committee, "Provisional Political Statement of the Prairie Fire Organizing Committee," *Breakthrough*, 1: 1, San Francisco, March 1977, p. 34.

6.   John Brown Book Club, ed., *The Split of the Weather Underground*, Seattle, 1977, p. 33.

7.   Ibid.

8.   Ibid., p. 35.

9.   Biskind, "Weather Underground Splits."

10.   Lee Lescaze, "Rudd Emerges from Underground and Surrenders," *Washington Post*, September 15, 1977, p. A2.

11.   JBAKC leaflet, anti-Klan demonstration 1978, Walnut Creek, California.

12.   See Shakur's book *Assata!*, Lawrence Hill, Wesport, Connecticut, 1978, for a detailed description of this episode.

13.   Margot Hornblower and James L. Rowe, "Out of the Underground," *Washington Post*, July 9, 1980, p. A1.

14.   Doug Kneeland, "Ex-Radical Leader Gets Probation and Fine in 1969 Chicago Protests," *New York Times*, January 14, 1981, p. 14.

15.   Robert Davis, "Days of Rage Now More Like a Convulsion that Became a Blip in History," *Chicago Tribune*, January 8, 1994, p. 6.

Bibliography

BOOKS

Albert, Judith Clavier and Stewart Albert, eds., *The Sixties Papers*, Praeger, New York, 1984.

Ali, Tariq, ed., *The New Revolutionaries: A Handbook of the International Radical Left*, William Morrow, New York, 1969.

Alpert, Jane, *Growing Up Underground*, Morrow, New York, 1981.

Aronowitz, Stanley, *Honor America: The Nature of Fascism, Historic Struggles against It, and a Strategy for Today*, Times Change Press, New York, 1970.

Attewell, Paul, *Radical Political Economics since the 1960s: A Sociology of Knowledge Analysis*, Rutgers University Press, New Brunswick, N.J., 1984.

Bowser, Benjamin and Raymond Hunt, eds., *Impacts of Racism on White America*, Sage, Beverly Hills, Cal., 1981.

Brown, H. Rap, *Die Nigger Die*, Dial Press, New York, 1969.

Carmichael, Stokeley and Charles Hamilton, *Black Power: The Politics of Liberation in America*, Vintage, New York, 1967.

Castellucci, John, *The Big Dance*, Dodd, Mead, New York, 1986.

Committee on the Judiciary, *Extent of Subversion in the "New Left"*, US Government Printing Office, Washington, D.C., 1974–5.

Daniels, Robert V., *Year of the Heroic Guerrilla: World Revolution and Counterrevolution in 1968*, Basic Books, New York, 1989.

Davis, Angela, and others, *If They Come In The Morning*, Signet, New American Library, Chicago, 1971.

Debray, Régis, *Revolution in the Revolution?*, Grove Press, New York, 1967.

Donner, Frank, *The Age of Surveillance*, Alfred Knopf, New York, 1980.

DuBoff, Richard, *Accumulation and Power: An Economic History of the United States*, M.E. Sharpe, Armonk, N.Y., 1989.

Fanon, Frantz, *The Wretched of the Earth*, Grove Press, New York, 1963.

Foner, Philip S., *U.S. Labor and the Vietnam War*, International Publishers, New York, 1989.

—— ed., *The Black Panthers Speak*, Lippincott, Philadelphia, 1970.

Fraser, Ronald, *1968: A Student Generation in Revolt*, Pantheon, New York, 1988.

Gitlin, Todd, *The Sixties: Years of Hope, Days of Rage*, Bantam, New York, 1987.

Glick, Brian, *The War at Home*, South End Press, Boston, 1989.

Grant, Joanne, *Confrontation on Campus: The Columbia Pattern for the New Protest*, New American Library, New York, 1969.

Grathwohl, Larry, *Bringing Down America: An FBI Informer with the Weathermen*, Arlington House, New Rochelle, N.Y., 1976.

Hayden, Tom, *The Trial*, Holt, Rinehart & Winston, New York, 1970.

Heath, Louis, ed., *Off the Pigs: The History and Literature of the*

Black Panther Party, Scarecrow Press, Metuchen, N.J., 1976.

—— *Vandals in the Bomb Factory: History and Literature of SDS*, Scarecrow Press, Metuchen, N.J., 1976.

Hilliard, David, *This Side of Glory*, Little, Brown, Boston, 1993.

Hurwitz, Ken, *Marching Nowhere*, Norton, New York, 1971.

Jacobs, Harold, ed., *Weatherman*, Ramparts Press, Berkeley, Cal., 1970.

Jackson, George, *Soledad Brother: The Prison Letters of George Jackson*, Bantam, New York, 1970.

Katsiaficas, George, *The Imagination of the New Left: A Global Analysis of 1968*, South End, Boston, 1987.

Kesey, Ken and Paul Krassner, eds., *The Last Supplement to the Whole Earth Catalog*, Whole Earth Catalog, Menlo Park, Cal., 1971.

Lader, Lawrence, *Power on the Left: American Radical Movements Since 1946*, Norton, New York, 1979.

Leary, Timothy, *Confessions of a Hope Fiend*, Bantam, New York, 1973.

Lee, Martin and Bruce Shlain, *Acid Dreams: The CIA, LSD, and the Sixties Rebellion*, Grove Press, New York, 1985.

Lenin, V.I., *Left-Wing Communism: An Infantile Disorder?*, International Publishers, New York, 1940.

Lewis, Roger, *Outlaws of America: The Underground Press and Its Context: Notes on a Cultural Revolution*, Penguin Books, Baltimore, 1972.

Malcolm X., *By Any Means Necessary*, Pathfinder Press, New York, 1970.

Marcuse, Herbert, *One Dimensional Man*, Beacon Press, Boston, 1964.

—— "Repressive Tolerance," in R. Wolff, B. Moore and H. Marcuse, *A Critique of Pure Tolerance*, Beacon Press, Boston, 1965.

Melville, Samuel, *Letters from Attica*, William Morrow, New York, 1972.

Morrison, Joan, and Robert K. Morrison, *From Camelot to Kent State: The Sixties Experience in the Words of Those Who Lived It*, Times Books, New York, 1987.

Nadelson, Regina, *Who Is Angela Davis? The Biography of a Revolutionary*, Peter H. Wyden, New York, 1972.

Newton, Huey, *Revolutionary Suicide*, Harcourt Brace Jovanovich, New York, 1973.

Oglesby, Carl, ed., *The New Left Reader*, Grove Press, New York, 1969.

Powers, Thomas, *Diana: The Making of a Terrorist*, Bantam, New York, 1971.

Prairie Fire Organizing Committee, *The Split of the Weather Underground Organization: Struggling against White and Male Supremacy*, John Brown Book Club, Seattle, 1977.

Raskin, Jonah, *Out of the Whale*, Links Books, New York, 1974.

Roszak, Theodore, *The Making of a Counter Culture*, Doubleday, Garden City, N.Y., 1975.

Sale, Kirkpatrick, *SDS*, Vintage, New York, 1973.

Select Committee to Study Government Operation with Respect to Intelligence Activities, *Supplementary Detailed Staff Reports on Intelligence Activities and the Rights of Americans, Book III, Final Report*, United States Government Printing Office, Washington, D.C., 1976.

Seale, Bobby, *Seize the Time*, Random House, New York, 1970.

Shakur, Assata, *Assata!*, Lawrence Hill, Westport, Conn., 1987.

Sojourn, Celia [alias], *Politics in Command*, John Brown Book Club, Seattle, 1975.

Spofford, Tim, *Lynch Street: The May 1970 Slayings at Jackson State*, Kent State University Press, Kent, Ohio, 1988.

Stern, Susan, *With the Weatherman*, Doubleday, Garden City, N.Y., 1975.

Stevens, Jay, *Storming Heaven: LSD and the American Dream*, Harper & Row, New York, 1987.

Taft, John, *Mayday at Yale: A Case Study in Student Radicalism*, Westview Press, Boulder, Col., 1976.

Thomas, Tom, *The Second Battle of Chicago: Chicago 1969*, Students for a Democratic Society, Grinnell, Iowa, 1969.

Union of Radical Political Economists, *U.S. Capitalism in Crisis*, Economic Education Project, New York, 1978.

Weather Underground Organization, *Prairie Fire: The Politics of Revolutionary Anti-Imperialism*, Communications Co., 1974.

Whitmer, Peter, *Aquarius Revisited*, Macmillan, New York, 1987.

Wicker, Tom, *A Time to Die*, Quadrangle/New York Times Book Co., New York, 1975.

ARTICLES

Biskind, Peter, "Weather Underground Splits on Whether to Go Overground," *SevenDays*, Institute for New Communications, Farmington, N.Y., February 28, 1977.

Breakthrough, San Francisco.

Bulletin of Concerned Asian Scholars, "The Vietnam Antiwar Movement in Perspective," vol. 21 (1989).

Gintis, H., "The New Working Class and Revolutionary Youth," *Socialist Revolution*, May–June 1970, Agenda Publishing, San Francisco.

Glusman, Paul, "More Mao Than Thou," *Ramparts*, Noah's Ark, Berkeley, Cal., September 1969.

Horowitz, D., and P. Collier, "Doing It," *Rolling Stone,* September 30, 1982.

Kopkind, Andrew, "Going Down in Chicago," *Hard Times,* New Weekly Project, Washington, D.C., October 20, 1969.

O'Brien, James, "Beyond Reminiscence: The New Left in History," *Radical America,* July 1972.

Ono, Shin'ya, "You Do Need a Weatherman to Know Which Way the Wind Blows," *Leviathan,* San Francisco, December 1969.

Weinstein, J., "Weatherman: A Lot of Thunder But a Short Reign," *Socialist Revolution,* 1:1 (January–February 1970).

FILM

DeAntonio, Emile, dir., *Underground,* with Mary Wexler and members of Weather Underground Organization, First Run Features, New York, 1976.

NEWSPAPERS

Berkeley Tribe, Berkeley Cal.

The Black Panther, Oakland, Cal.

Chicago Seed, Chicago, Ill.

Chicago Tribune, Chicago, Ill.

City Star, New York (prior to 1972, *Liberated Guardian*).

Dock Of the Bay, San Francisco, Cal.

Eugene Augur, Eugene, Oregon.

FIRE! (The Fire Next Time), Chicago, Ill.

Georgia Straight, Vancouver, B.C.
Guardian, New York.
Helix, Seattle, Washington.
Liberated Guardian, New York.
Liberation News Service, Washington, D.C.
New Left Notes, Chicago, Ill.
Old Mole, Boston, Mass.
Osawatomie, Seattle, Washington.
New York Times, New York.
Portland Scribe, Portland, Oregon.
Quicksilver Times, Washington, D.C.
Rat, New York.
Rising Up Angry, Chicago, Ill.
RYM, Southern California.
San Francisco Good Times, San Francisco, Cal.
Sedition, San Jose, Cal.
Takeover, Madison, Wis.
Workers World, New York.

A Weather Chronology

1968

January	Tet offensive in Vietnam; US embassy in Saigon attacked; demonstrations against Secretary of State Dean Rusk in New York and San Francisco; Oakland 7 indicted.
February	Police kill three black students and wound more than thirty others in Orangeburg, South Carolina, during sit-ins to desegregate lunch counters.
March 31	President Lyndon B. Johnson announces he won't seek a second term.
April 4	Martin Luther King, Jr., is murdered, sparking nationwide rebellions in urban neighborhoods.
April 6	Black Panther Bobby Hutton is killed by Oakland police.
Late April–May	Columbia University uprising; student–worker insurrection in France.
June 6	Robert Kennedy murdered.
Late August	Soviet Union invades Czechoslovakia; Democratic Convention in Chicago; Yippie Festival of Life.

November	Richard M. Nixon elected president.
December	"Towards a Revolutionary Youth Movement" proposal presented at SDS national convention in Ann Arbor.

1969

March	Chicago 8 indicted.
May	People's Park uprising in Berkeley, California.
June 18	"You Don't Need a Weatherman" published in *New Left Notes*.
June 20	SDS splits into Progressive Labor and anti-Progressive Labor factions; Revolutionary Youth Movement (RYM) and Weatherman are born.
July–August	During organizing in July for October National Action, RYM and Weatherman break ranks; in August, organizing continues for two different actions (Weatherman's will become known as Days of Rage); RYM is now RYM II.
August 19	Black Panther Bobby Seale is arrested in Berkeley and transported to Chicago for trial.
August 24–8	Woodstock Festival in upstate New York.
September	Chicago 8 trial begins.
October 7	Weather blows up Haymarket police statue in Chicago.
October 8–12	Days of Rage in Chicago; RYM II actions.
October 15	Millions protest war in Vietnam during the National Moratorium Against the War.
November 15	National Mobilization to End the War – a million demonstrate in Washington D.C., over 200,000 in San Francisco; clashes with police occur in D.C. in marches on South Vietnamese embassy and the Justice Department.
November 16	MyLai massacre made public.

December 4	Black Panthers Fred Hampton and Mark Clark murdered by police in Chicago.
Mid-December	Weather firebombs Chicago police cars in retaliation for Hampton/Clark murders.
Late December	Flint war council; Weatherman decides to go underground.

1970

January	Silas and Judith Bissell of Seattle Weather attempt to bomb the University of Washington Reserve Officers Training Corps building; both are arrested.
February	All women's issue of *Rat* published, which includes Robin Morgan's feminist statement "Goodbye to All That."
February 16	The Day After (TDA) protests occur across US after the convictions in the Chicago Conspiracy Trial (Chicago 8[7]).
February 19	Timothy Leary convicted on marijuana charges.
March 6	Townhouse explosion in New York City – three Weather members die, two escape; FBI dragnet intensifies.
March 17	First federal indictments from Days of Rage released.
April 15	Linda Evans arrested on Days of Rage indictment.
April 23	"Free Bobby Seale and Ericka Huggins" week of actions in New Haven, Connecticut.
April 30	Nixon announces invasion of Cambodia; campuses, youth ghettoes, even military bases across the country and in Europe erupt in massive protests; nationwide student strike begins.
May 4	Four students murdered and many others wounded by National Guard at Kent State University, Ohio.
May 9	Some 200,000 demonstrate in Washington, D.C., against the invasion of Cambodia and domestic repression.

May 14	Two students murdered by police at Jackson State University, Mississippi, during an anti-war demonstration.
Late May	Weather bombs the National Guard headquarters in Washington, D.C.
Mid-June	Weather bombs the headquarters of the New York Police Department.
July 23	New indictments issued against 13 Weather members.
July 26	Weather bombs the Presidio Army Base in San Francisco.
August 7	Jonathan Jackson and others attempt to free Soledad Brothers from the Marin County courthouse; he and three others die in shootout with police and guards.
August 24	Army Math Research Center bombed by New Year's Gang in Madison, Wisconsin; one graduate student dies.
September 13	Weather helps Timothy Leary escape from prison.
October	Angela Davis arrested on conspiracy charges related to Marin County courthouse escape attempt; Weather detonates bombs at the Marin County courthouse; Weather sets off bombs in three cities – Chicago, Long Island, and Cambridge.
December 6	"New Morning" communiqué mailed to Liberation News Service and published in underground newspapers across the country.
December 16	Judy Clark arrested on Days of Rage indictments.
Winter 1970–71	People's Peace Treaty made public.

1971

March	Bomb explodes in US Capitol building in opposition to the escalating war in Laos.
Early Spring	Black Panthers split over politics and the necessity of

armed struggle – New York chapter aligns with Cleaver's international wing, Newton continues to lead Oakland branch.

April 24–May 6	Massive demonstrations in Washington, D.C., against the war (organizers include New Mobilization to End the War in Vietnam, Vietnam Veterans Against the War, and the Mayday Tribe); martial law declared in D.C., over 12,000 arrested.
May 25	All charges dropped against Ericka Huggins and Bobby Seale.
August 21	George Jackson murdered at San Quentin.
Late August	Weather bombs California prison offices in San Francisco.
September 9–13	Attica State Penitentiary prison uprising and massacre.
Late September	Weather bombs New York Commissioner of Corrections offices in Albany, New York.
October	Weather bombs the Massachusetts Institute of Technology offices of Vietnam war architect McGeorge Bundy.
December	US intensifies bombing of northern Vietnam.

1972

May	US mines northern Vietnamese harbors and intensifies bombing of countryside; protests break out worldwide; on May 19, Weather explodes bomb in Pentagon.
June	Angela Davis acquitted; Watergate breakin and arrests.
August 1	President Nixon renominated at the Republican Convention amidst massive demonstrations in Miami Beach, Florida.
November	Richard M. Nixon elected president'for a second term.

Late December	US carpetbombs Vietnam in what becomes known as the Christmas bombings; the Justice Department issues new indictments against Weather.

1973

January	Peace treaty signed between US and North Vietnam; war continues.
January 27	Draft ends.
March	American Indian Movement and allies begin defense of Wounded Knee against US Army and marshalls.
September	CIA–ITT sponsored coup in Chile – hundreds murdered, thousands arrested.
Late September	Weather bombs ITT Latin America offices.
October	Some federal indictments against Weather dropped because of illegal surveillance.
December	Vice President Agnew resigns and is replaced by Congressman Gerald Ford.

1974

February 4	Symbionese Liberation Army (SLA) kidnaps newspaper heiress Patty Hearst.
March 7	WUO bombs San Francisco Health, Education, and Welfare offices.
May 4	Six members of SLA killed in shoot-out with police in Compton, California.
May 9	Impeachment hearings begin against President Nixon.
Summer–Fall	*Prairie Fire: The Politics of Revolutionary Anti-Imperialism* released and distributed; film *Underground* released.
August 9	President Nixon resigns from the presidency.
September 8	President Ford pardons Nixon.

1975

January 23	Weather bombs government offices in Washington, D.C., and Oakland, California.
June 16	Weather bombs Banco de Ponce offices in New York City.
Summer	*Osawatamie* begins publication.
October 10	Weather bombs Kennecott Corporation headquarters in Salt Lake City, Utah.

1976

January 30–February 2	Hard Times conference in Chicago.
Spring–Summer	Weather divides into Central Committee and Revolutionary Committee over issues of race, gender, and organizational approaches.
November	Jimmy Carter elected president.
Late December	Revolutionary Committee expels Central Committee; Revolutionary Committee takes over WUO mantle.

1977

February 3	WUO (RC) bombs San Francisco Immigration and Naturalization Service offices.
March	Prairie Fire Organizing Committee publishes first issue of journal, *Breakthrough*.
September	Mark Rudd surrenders to authorities in New York.
November	Five WUO members arrested for conspiracy to bomb California State Senator John Briggs's office.
1977–80	John Brown Anti-Klan Committee formed; some former Weather members join May 19 Organization or PFOC; most remain underground.

1980

July	Cathy Wilkerson surfaces in New York.

November	Ronald Reagan elected president.
December	Bill Ayers and Bernardine Dohrn surface in New York.

1981–88

October 1981	Jeff Jones and Eleanor Raskin are arrested in New York; Black Liberation Army and May 19 Organization botch hold-up of Brinks armored truck; Boudin, Gilbert, and Clark are among those arrested; two police, one security guard, and one BLA member die.
Early 1980s	The PFOC are active in movements against US war in Central America; in solidarity with Puerto Rican *independentistas*; against apartheid; and continue publishing *Breakthrough*; Armed Resistance Unit (ARU) formed (January).
November 7, 1983	ARU bombs US Capitol building in protest against US invasion of Grenada.
November 1984	President Reagan reelected.
Fall 1985	Linda Evans and Laura Whitehorn arrested for Capitol bombing.
1987	Silas Bissell arrested after seventeen years underground.
November 1988	George Bush elected president.

1991–94

1991	US goes to war in Persian Gulf in January; demonstrations occur worldwide. War ends in March.
November 1992	Bill Clinton elected president.
January 6 1994	Jeff Powell, a foot soldier in the Days of Rage, surrenders in Chicago to face riot charges after nearly twenty-five years underground.

The Cast

Bill Ayers was the son of the chairman of the utility corporation, Commonwealth Edison, of Chicago. His first political arrest came at a sit-in at an Ann Arbor draft board in October 1965. He met Diana Oughton later that school year, and together they began working at the Children's Community School. This alternative school for disadvantaged youngsters soon ran into trouble because of the trustees' differences with Bill and Diana's radical politics and the fact that they were living together outside marriage. After the school folded, the two became very involved with Ann Arbor SDS. Ayers was a founding member of Weatherman and prominent in the leadership until his departure in 1977. He surfaced with Bernardine Dohrn in 1980.

Silas Bissell was an heir to the carpet-cleaner magnate's fortune. He and his then wife Judith were indicted on charges of attempting to bomb the ROTC building at the University of

Washington in 1970. Both went underground and separated from each other. Judith stayed with the WUO until her arrest in 1977. Silas was finally arrested after several years underground in 1987 and served two years.

Kathy Boudin became involved in SDS through its community-organizing project ERAP. She was one of the founding members of Weather, escaped alive from the townhouse explosion, and stayed with the group to the end. She went underground after the explosion and was finally arrested (as a member of the May 19 Communist Organization) after the failed Brinks holdup attempt in Nyack, N.Y., and was sentenced to twenty years to life for her role. Her father was the famed civil-rights lawyer Leonard Boudin. She is currently serving time in a New York prison facility and is active in AIDS counseling and prisoner rights.

Judy Clark joined SDS in 1965 and the *New Left Notes* staff shortly thereafter. She participated in the Days of Rage and the preceding organizational actions, and was listed in the original federal indictments. She was one of the few ever arrested on those charges during Weather's heyday. She served seven months in prison and worked as an aboveground ally after her release. In 1981 she was arrested for her involvement in the BLA/May 19 Organization Brinks holdup attempt. She is currently serving seventy-five years to life in New York prisons.

Bernardine Dohrn was raised in a middle-class suburb of Milwaukee, Wisconsin, and, after college, went to law school in Chicago. She moved to New York, finding employment as a paralegal. She joined SDS and was national secretary in

1968–9. A founding member of Weatherman, it was usually her signature which appeared on Weather communiqués. Dohrn was probably the best-known of all the Weather people and its primary spokesperson. She left the organization in 1977 and surfaced in 1980.

Jennifer Dohrn, Bernardine's sister, served as aboveground support for Weather until Bernardine left the organization. She was instrumental in the publication and distribution of *Prairie Fire: The Politics of Revolutionary Anti-Imperialism*.

Linda Evans joined SDS in 1967. She was one of the delegation of US anti-imperialists and peace activists who went to Hanoi in 1969 to receive prisoners of war released by the Vietnamese. She was charged in the first of several indictments stemming from the Days of Rage, and spent some time in the early 1970s in prison. After the dissolution of WUO, she worked with the John Brown Anti-Klan Committee in Texas for a few years and then moved east where she became involved in clandestine work through the Armed Resistance Unit. Following the Capitol bombing in November 1983, she spent several months on the lam before she was arrested in Baltimore, Maryland, with other members of the organization. She is currently serving forty years to life.

Dave Gilbert was one of those involved in the anti-IDA work at Columbia University preceding the April–May 1968 rebellion. He had been involved earlier with the civil-rights group CORE and in protests against the Navy ROTC branch at Columbia, and was almost expelled for his acts in the latter. In mid-1968 he committed himself to political work, joining Weatherman at its inception and moving underground after the Flint war council. He continued underground activities as a member of Weather and the May 19 Organization until his arrest after the Nyack Brinks holdup attempt in 1981. He is now serving seventy-five years to life for his role in that action.

John Jacobs (known as JJ) was a former PL member well read in communist revolutionary theory. A founding member of Weatherman and part of the original leadership, he drifted away from the organization in the early 1970s. (He is no relation of the author.)

Naomi Jaffe worked with New York SDS. In 1968, Bernardine Dohrn and Jaffe wrote "You Got the Look," one of the first feminist viewpoints to be published in *New Left Notes*. She was a founding member of Weatherman and remained with the organization into the 1970s.

Jeff Jones, originally from California, worked for a year or two in the New York regional office of SDS. He was a student at Antioch College, a progressive university in Yellow Springs, Ohio, prior to moving to New York. Jeff was an early spokesperson for Weather and a founding member. He remained with the organization throughout the 1970s and left when the programs he, Ayers, Dohrn, and others had sponsored were discredited. He was arrested in 1981 along with Eleanor Raskin.

Mike Klonsky joined SDS in 1966 at San Fernando State College in Southern California. He participated in a demonstration/teach-in at a military base and was arrested. Klonsky was one of the primary authors of the RYM statements of December 1968. He split with SDS/Weather in August 1969 and helped organize several multiracial youth coalitions and organizations against the war and for revolutionary change, including RYM2 and the October League.

Jim Mellen was already in his thirties in 1968 and had been actively involved in the May 2nd Movement (M2M) – an anti-war, anti-imperialist organization top-heavy with Progressive Labor Party members. In addition to his participation in M2M, Mellen was secretary-treasurer of the New York Free University in fall, 1965 and taught courses in Marx, Lenin, Mao, and other communist revolutionaries. Upon his arrival in Ann Arbor, Mellen joined the SDS Radical Education Project (REP). Although a founding member of Weatherman, he left after the war council of December 1969.

Jeff Powell was a laborer in Illinois who was arrested during the Days of Rage on mob-action charges. He went underground immediately and worked in homeless shelters and other non-profit-making organizations. He remained underground until surrendering in Chicago in 1994.

Eleanor Raskin was born into a leftist family and joined the civil-rights and anti-war struggles early on. She was married to Jonah Raskin for a couple of years, but after the Columbia uprising went her own way. She co-authored *The Bust Book* with Kathy Boudin in 1967. Eleanor signed on early with Weather and stayed until the organization split. She was arrested with her partner, Jeff Jones, in October 1981.

Mark Rudd joined Columbia SDS in late autumn of 1966 after an SDS campaign against CIA recruiting on campus. In 1967, he was arrested at a sit-in in the same cause. He grew up in

Maplewood, a New Jersey suburb where his father sold real estate and served as a lieutenant colonel in the Army reserves. He was a founding member of Weather, but drifted away from the organization in the early 1970s. He surfaced in 1977.

Susan Stern graduated from college as a debutante, married, and moved to Seattle with her husband Robby. She first encountered SDS in 1967, at a New Politics convention in Chicago. Her first political demonstration, however, was against sexism. She left Robby in the winter of 1967–8, went to Berkeley, then to Los Angeles, where she worked for SDS. In August 1968, she attended the Democratic Convention in Chicago. She joined Weather at its inception and left in early 1970. She then helped form the Seattle Liberation Front, an anti-imperialist group, and was arrested on conspiracy charges along with seven other Seattle activists after a violent demonstration against the verdicts in the Chicago 7 trial. These eight became known as the Seattle 8.

Clayton van Lydegraf was, by the time he met up with Weather, a man in his sixties. Coming of age during the Russian Revolution, he worked with various Left organizations throughout his life. In early 1960 he was expelled from the Communist Party – USA (along with several other members) over differences arising from the Sino-Soviet split. Together with others who had been expelled, he helped form the Maoist Progressive Labor Party. Later in the decade he was expelled from PL. Van Lydegraf worked with Weather members until his arrest with four other members in 1977. He died in 1992.

Cathy Wilkerson was raised a Quaker in the midwest. Her

political history began when she attended a sit-in to desegregate a lunch counter in Cambridge, Maryland. She graduated from Swarthmore College in 1966 and immersed herself in the anti-war movement. As a member of SDS she traveled to Hanoi and eventually helped create Weatherman. She was indicted for her actions during the Days of Rage and, when she went underground, forfeited $40,000 bail. With Kathy Boudin, she survived the townhouse blast. Cathy surfaced in 1980 and served two years in prison.

Index

Note: Page references for illustrations are italicized.

Agency for International
    Development (USAID) bomb
    170–1
Agnew, Spiro T. 106
Albert, Judith (Gumbo) 119
Albert, Stew 70, 119
Alpert, Jane 144–5
American Indian Movement 116
Ashley, Karin
    birth of Weather 25
Attica Liberation Faction 138–9
Attica State Penitentiary 136, 138–40
Avakian, Bob 174
Ayers, Bill
    SDS days 7, 14, 16
    youth culture and class 20–1
    birth of Weather 25, 26
    national office 39
    revolution not adventurism 53–4
    community school 99
    indicted 100, 114
    nervousness 117
    life underground 144
    writing of Prairie Fire 158
    Weather split 175
    life with Bernardine and children
        182
    May 19 Organization 182
    surrenders 184
    against war in Iraq 186
    biography 203

Bacon, Leslie 135
Banco de Ponce bomb 171
Bank of America bomb 109
Bissell, Judith 175, 180, 203–4
Bissell, Silas 186, 203–4
Black Liberation Army
    support from May 19 Organization
        182–3
    Brinks holdup 185–6
Black Panther Party
    confrontation and organizing 7
    most revolutionary 12–13
    repression 21
    at odds with PL 25–6, 39
    Weather support 28–9
    raid on Chicago office 32
    Chicago action 53, 61
    criticism of Weather in Chicago 68
    aims 69
    Clark and Hampton killed 83–4,
        86
    bombing conspiracy trial 98, 102

out of favor with Weather 104
federal target 116
warnings about drugs 128
change of attitude and factions
    131–2
Soledad Brothers 136
community efforts 153
Black Power (Carmichael) 28
Bolivar, Simon 34
Boston University 48
Boudin, Kathy
    birth of Weather 27
    committee organization 39
    New York bomb explosion 95–9
    indicted 100, 114
    life underground 145
    Weather split 175
    May 19 Organization 182
    Brinks holdup 185
    biography 204
Bread and Roses collective 91–2
Breakthrough (journal) 175–7
Brewster, Kingman 101
Briggs, Senator John 179–80
Brinks holdup 185–6
Brown, Benjamin 48
Brown, H. Rap 104
Brown, Sam 185
Buck, Marilyn J. 186
Burlingham, Robert 114

Cabral, Amilcar 46
Cambodia 104
Capitol building bomb 129–30, 135
Carmichael, Stokely
    Black Power 28
Carter, Jimmy 181
CASA 172
Castro, Fidel 34
Chase Manhattan Bank bomb 82
Chicago
    preparation for 1969 convergence
        51, 53–4
    1969 action 54–64
    subsequent evaluation 66–7
Chicago Democratic Convention 18
Chicago 8 41

attend Weather action in Chicago
    55
rally outside courthouse 61
convictions 94–5
Chile 171
Christmas, William 120–1
Clapp, Peter 180–1
Clark, Judy 124–5
    indicted 100
    May 19 Organization 182
    Brinks holdup 185
    biography 204
Clark, Matt 84, 86
Class War comix 72
Cleaver, Eldridge
    support from afar 67–8, 104, 119
    disagreement with Newton faction
        132
Clutchette, John 120
Columbia Records 107
Columbia University 32
    race relations 8
    uprising 8–12
Counter Intelligence Program 74
Crowley, Walt 104

Daley, Mayor Richard 3, 18
Davidson, Carl
    Vietnamese heroes 49
    criticism of Weather 70–1
    on *Prairie Fire* 168
Davis, Angela 122, 136
Davis, Rennie 133
Dean, John 116
Debray, Régis
    Revolution in the Revolution? 34–7
Defense Department, Oakland, bomb
    170–1
DeFreeze, Donald 150
Delgado, Marion 56
Dohrn, Bernardine 12, *63*
    "White Mother Country Radicals"
        13
    feminist strategy 22
    birth of Weather 25, 26
    black struggle as fight against
        imperialism 27

committee organization 39
Cuban tour 50–1
leads march on Chicago draft
    board 60–1
on Chicago 66
on Manson murders 87
indicted 100, 114
response to Cambodia 106
Leary escape 118
new morning, changing weather
    122–4
life underground 144–5, 182
writing of *Prairie Fire* 158–9
Weather split 175
criticizes self and committee for
    selling out 177–8
May 19 Organization 182
surrenders 184
biography 204–5
Dohrn, Jennifer 124, 205
publication of *Prairie Fire* 160, 167
Hard Times conference 172–3
baby kidnap plot 179
Donghi, Dianne 101, *115*
Cuban tour 50–1
arrest 108, 109, 114
Donner, Frank 74
Drumgo, Fleeta 120
Duarte, José Napoleón 183
Dylan, Bob
"Subterranean Homesick Blues"
    24–5
"New Morning" 127

Elrod, Richard 62
Evans, Linda 86
indicted and arrested 100–1
arrest 107–8, 109, 114
May 19 Organization 182
later arrest 185–6
biography 205

Federal Bureau of Investigation 73,
    107–8
FIRE! 75, 76
Flanagan, Brian 62, *63*
Fliegelman, Ronald 114

Fortner, Grace 180
Froines, John 55
Fuerst, John 146, 181
Furst, Randy 70–1

General Electric 75
General Motors bomb 82
Gilbert, Dave
Weather split 175
May 19 Organization 182
Brinks holdup 185
biography 205–6
Glusman, Paul 29
Gold, Ted 106
Columbia protest 9
Cuban tour 50–1
killed in bomb explosion 95–100
Grabiner, Vicky 94
Grathwohl, Larry 73, 94, 146
recruitment 49–50
cover blown 107–8
named in indictment 114
Gray Panthers 172
Guardian collective 70–1
Guevara, Che 34
Gulf Oil bomb 158

Haley, Judge 120–1
Hampton, Fred 53, 84, 86
Handelsman, Leonard 146
Hard Times conference 170, 171–4
racism and sexism 173–4
Harvard University 48, 74
bomb at Center for International
    Affairs 122
Hayden, Tom 41, 55
defense of revolution 69–70
Haymarket Square bombs 54, 121
Hearst, Patricia 149–50, 154
Hearst, William 150
Hilliard, David 29
Hirsch, Phoebe 180–1
Ho Chi Minh 143, 182
New Year Greetings 1–2
Hoffman, Abbie 18, 41, 55, 70
Hoffman, Anita 18
Hoffman, Judge Julius 100, 125, 150

Hoover, J. Edgar 116
Huggins, Ericka 101, 105, 135
Huston, John 116

Institute for Defense Analysis (IDA)
    8–9

Jackson, George 120–1, 122
    circumstances of death 136–7
Jackson, Jonathan 120–1, 122
Jackson, Terry 186
Jackson State College killings 105
Jacobs, Harold 40
Jacobs, John 9
    birth of Weather 25
    indicted 100
    biography 206
Jaffe, Naomi
    feminism 22
    indicted 114
    biography 206
Jesse James Gang 7, 14
John Brown Anti-Klan Committee
    182–3
Jones, Jeff 207
    birth of Weather 25, 26
    control of Students for a
        Democratic Society (SDS)
        39–40
    on strategy of fighting police 57, 60
    arrested in Haymarket Square 62
    indicted 100
    writing of Prairie Fire 158
    Weather split 175
    life with Raskin and child 182
    May 19 Organization 182
    later arrest 184–5
    biography 206
Justesen, Mike T. 175, 179–80

Kalman, Tibor 88
Kanter, Paul 127
Kennecott Corporation bomb 171
Kent State University killings 105
King Jr, Martin Luther 3
Kirk, Grayson 8
Kissinger, Henry 130, 183

Klonsky, Mike
    "Towards a Revolutionary Youth
        Movement" 19–21
    resignation 39, 40
    biography 206–7
Kopkind, Andrew 67
Krassner, Paul 18
Kurshan, Nancy 18

Labor Committees 168
Laos 129–30
LaRouche, Lyndon 168
Leary, Timothy
    freed from prison by Weather
        117–20
Lefcourt, Mark 114
Lennon, John 107
    "The Dream is Over" (with Ono)
        162
Lindsay, John 121
Long, Gerry 25
Long Island court building bomb 121

McCarthy, Eugene 18
McClain, James 120–1
McGovern, George 141–2
Machtinger, Howie 147
    birth of Weather 25
    indicted 100
Mad Dogs 119
Magee, Ruchell 120
Malcolm X 182
Mann, Eric 48, 74
Manson, Charles 87, 91, 93
Marcuse, Herbert 5
Marin County Courthouse
    bomb 120–1
    shooting 136
May 2nd Movement 3–4
May 19 Communist Organization
    181–3
Mayday Tribe 131, 132–3, 135
Mayday (1971) Week 132–5
Mellen, Jim 7, 87
    youth culture and class 20–1
    birth of Weather 25
    biography 207

Mitchell, John 133
Mobilization to End the War 75, 82, 83
Morgan, Robin 90
Murphy, Red 167

National Labor Party 168
National Liberation Front of Vietnam 49
National Organizing Committee 39
National Peace Action Coalition 141
Neufeld, Russel 109, 114
New American Movement 168
New Left Notes
    "Resistance and Repression" 4
Newton, Huey P. 101
    on white radicals 24
    demonstrations of support 39
    criticism of Weather in Chicago 68
    disagreement with Cleaver faction 132
New World Liberation Front 169
New York City Police Headquarters bomb 109
Niles, Phil 48
Nixon, Richard M. 130, 145
    bombs Cambodia 104
    domestic killings and withdrawal from Cambodia 105
    suppression 106–7
    Huston plan to destroy Left 116–17
    Watergate scandal 162

October League 168
Olson, Henry 48
Ono, Shin'ya 56
    on Chicago 66
Ono, Yoko
    "The Dream is Over" (with Lennon) 162
Organization of Petroleum Exporting Countries (OPEC) 163
Osawatomie 170
Oswald, Russell 140
Oughton, Diana *16*, *80*, 106, 203
    Cuban tour 50–1
    killed in bomb explosion 95–100
    song for 127–8

Pentagon bomb 142
People's Coalition for Peace and Justice 131, 141
People's Park, Berkeley 31–2
Perry, Marc 175, 179–80
Powell, Jeff 186, 207
Prairie Fire Organizing Committee *159*, 170, 182–3
    Hard Times conference 171–4
    Weather splinters 174–8
    attacks and arrests 185–6
Prairie Fire 146
    opening statement 157–8
    role of Left in revolutionary struggle 160–2, 164–5
    on imperialism 162–4
    women and feminism 165–7
    response to publication 167–9
    Dohrn criticizes self and others for 177–8
Presidio Army base bomb 109
Progressive Labor Party
    divisions within SDS 3–4
    educational approach 7
    racism and drugs 20
    Black Panthers' tirade against 25–6
    creates division 37
    at odds with Panthers 39
Puerto Rican Socialist Party 172
Puerto Rico 171

Raskin, Eleanor 206
    Cuban tour 50–1
    life with Jones and child 182
    arrested 184–5
    biography 207
Rat
    women speak out 91, 92–3
RCA 107
Real, Mark, 146
Reilly, Ro 167
Reserve Officers Training Corps (ROTC)
    buildings trashed 51, 105
Revolutionary Communist Party 174, 183
Revolutionary Unions 168

Revolutionary Youth Movement 21, 26
    control of SDS 38–9
    Chicago 1969 action 53, 61, 62
    tactics 70–1
Revolution in the Revolution? (Debray)
    34–7
Robbins, Terry 7, 106
    birth of Weather 25, 27
    committee organization 39–40
    fighting talk 42
    killed in bomb explosion 95–100
Rockefeller, Nelson 138, 139
Roth, Robert
    surrender 180–1
Rubin, Jerry 18, 41
Rudd, Mark
    aligning with the oppressed 8
    Columbia protest 9, *10*
    birth of Weather 25, 26
    boasts about lack of reading 34
    control of Students for a
        Democratic Society (SDS)
        39–40
    fighting talk 42
    priest and hangman playing pig 46,
        48
    arrested in Haymarket Square 62
    feels like Captain Ahab 85
    indicted 100, 114
    Leary escape 118
    life underground 144
    asked to leave 145
    surrenders 180, 184
    biography 207–8
Rusk, Dean 4–5, 9

Sacramento prison 137
Sale, Kirkpatrick 34
San Francisco Immigration and
    Naturalization Office bomb 178
San Francisco state prison 137
San Mateo prison 137
Seale, Bobby 95, 101, 105, 135
Seattle 8 208
Seattle uprising 41
Senate Committee of Internal
    Security 73

Shakur, Assata 182
Sinclair, John 107
Slick, Grace 127
Smith, Roberta 146, 181
Sojourn, Celia (pseudonym) 158
Soledad Brothers 120–1, 122, 136
Spiegel, Mark 100
Spiegelman, Jane 114, *115*
Standard Oil bomb 82
Stern, Susan 21–2, 87, 208
Student Nonviolent Coordinating
    Committe (SNCC) 7
Students for a Democratic Society
    (SDS)
    internal divisions 3–4
    moral versus political approach 6
    internationalist conscience 7–8
    nationalism and national liberation
        13
    support for Eugene McCarthy 18
    attempts to broaden to working
        class 18–21
    feminism 21–2
    convention of 1969 and birth of
        Weatherman 24–7
    PL creates division 37
    call for 1969 day of action 38–9
    breaking sexual monogamy 45–6
    aim to rebuild 87
Sundiata, Mtayari 185
Swartout, Robert 114
Symbionese Liberation Army 149–51,
    152, 169
    police siege 154

Takeover (newspaper) 167–8
Tappis, Steve 25
Tupamaro solution 60

United Black Workers 172

van Lydegraf, Clayton 146, 178
    publication of *Prairie Fire* 160
    goes underground 170
    Weather split 175
    Briggs plan 179–80
    biography 208

Vietnam Veterans Against the War 133, 141
Vietnam war 130
  SDS reactions to 3–6
  nationalism 13
  draft issues 19
  National Liberation Front as heroes 49
  Cuban tour 50–1
  Mobilization to End the War 75, 82
  escalation in 1972 and protests 140–4
  peace negotiations 143–4
  Hard Times Conference 172

Wald, Karen 5
Watergate scandal 162
Weather Organization
  and working class 39–40, 42-5, 71, 75
  birth at convention 24–7
  identification with black struggle 27–9
  united-front politics and youth movement 29–33
  Debray's influence 34–7
  control of SDS 38–9
  Motor City group leaves 43–4
  the draft and soldiers 49
  recruitment 49–50
  Cuban tour 50–1
  revolution not adventurism 53–4
  Chicago 1969 action 54–64
  escalate confrontation 57, 60–4
  aim for revolution 67–73
  government attempts to destroy 73–4, 106–17
  ideological struggle leads underground 84–5, 86–8
  and working class 87, 173–4
  feminism 90–3, 123–5
  underground and bombs 93–9
  indictments after townhouse bomb 100–1
  Panthers out of favor 104
  actions against Cambodian invasion 104–8
  begins bombing campaign 108–9
  frees Leary 117–20
  strategy beyond bombs 120, 122–5
  changing weather 127–32
  attack on California prisons 137–40
  bomb the New York prison offices 139–40
  Pentagon bomb 142–3
  Chile reaction 147–8
  later rhetoric of personal freedom and feminism 152–4
  builds Prairie Fire above ground 170
  split between east and west coasts 174–8
  Briggs plan leads to arrests 179–?0
  east coast forms May 19 Communist Organization 181–3
Weiss, Lawrence 100
Whitehorn, Laura 167, 186
Wilkerson, Cathy
  working-class toughs 42
  New York bomb explosion 95–9
  indicted 114
  life underground 145
  surrenders 183–4
  biography 208–9
Williams, Robert 27
Women's Brigade 151, 166
Wood, Michael P. 74–5
Woodstock festival 42

Yale University 101, 105
Yippies 18, 128
  aims 69, 70, 71, 73
  called before grand jury 131
Young Lords 53, 61, 128
  community efforts 153
Youth Against War and Fascism 172

Zimbabwe African National Union 172

Printed in the United States
by Baker & Taylor Publisher Services